In Bed with the Word

READING, SPIRITUALITY, AND CULTURAL POLITICS

In Bed with the Word

READING, SPIRITUALITY, AND CULTURAL POLITICS

The University of Alberta Press

DANIEL COLEMAN

Published by
The University of Alberta Press
Ring House 2
Edmonton, Alberta, Canada T6G 2E1

LIBRARY AND ARCHIVES CANADA CATALOGUING IN PUBLICATION

Coleman, Daniel, 1961–
    In bed with the word : reading, spirituality, and cultural politics / Daniel Coleman.

Includes bibliographical references and index.
ISBN 978-0-88864-507-4

    1. Books and reading—Religious aspects. 2. Books and reading—Sociological aspects.
3. Spirituality. I. Title.

Z1003.C75 2009   028   C2008-907117-4

The University of Alberta Press is committed to protecting our natural environment. As part of
our efforts, this book is printed on Enviro Paper: it contains 100% post-consumer recycled fibres
and is acid- and chlorine-free.

The University of Alberta Press gratefully acknowledges the support received for its publishing
program from The Canada Council for the Arts. The University of Alberta Press also gratefully
acknowledges the financial support of the Government of Canada through the Book Publishing
Industry Development Program (BPIDP) and from the Alberta Foundation for the Arts for its
publishing activities.

*To Wendy
with thanks for a lifelong companionship
in spirit and in word*

*To my parents,
Murray and Bea Coleman,
for introducing me to the importance
of Quiet Time*

CONTENTS

ACKNOWLEDGEMENTS

Certain authors, speaking of their works, say, "My book," "My commentary," "My history," etc. They resemble middle-class people who have a house of their own and always have "My house" on their tongue. They would do better to say, "Our book," "Our commentary," "Our history,"' etc., because there is in them usually more of other people's than their own.

—BLAISE PASCAL, Pensées, *p. 15–16*

SO MANY PEOPLE have contributed to this book that it does, indeed, feel very much like "our book." While they cannot be blamed for the limitations of my perspectives or my writing skills, I want to thank many people for their input. Catherine Bush, David Chariandy, Wendy Coleman, Donald Goellnicht, David Gray, Lori Kerr, Travis Kroeker, Julie McGonegal, Mary O'Connor, Jim Peck, Michael Ross, and John Terpstra read parts of the manuscript and/or discussed their ideas about it with me. I am grateful to Agnes Kramer-Hamstra, who gave the manuscript a crucial and meticulous "cold edit" when deadlines were looming. My perspectives on matters of the spiritual life have been indelibly shaped by family members, who, as this book indicates, set my early foundations in spiritual life, as well as by life-anchoring friendships with Timothy Bascom, Donald Goellnicht, Susan Chang Hong, Barbara and Paul Mutch, Gary and Carla Nelson, Gary and Joy Warner, and Cam and Joan Yates. I am fortunate to have such a wide circle of gifted friends who can offer good advice and clear insights. To this circle I would add the larger group of friends I have never met who wrote the books that animate every page I have written here.

This book has also benefited from the responses and inter-actions I received at three post-secondary institutions. Early versions of its chapters were the basis of a lecture series I presented at the Canadian Mennonite University and the University of Winnipeg in February 2005. I am grateful espe-cially to Paul Dyck and Chris Huebner, both faculty members at CMU, who hosted me there. I am thankful to Carol Wood who invited me to present a reading from this material for the McMaster Ecumenical Chaplaincy in November 2004 and to Liz Koblyk who invited me to give a talk in the McMaster Alumni lecture series in Winter 2005. Finally, I was deeply honoured to serve as Father Peter Nash S.J. Visiting Chair in Religion at Campion College, University of Regina, in Winter 2008, where I presented the Nash lecture and offered an undergraduate class, both based on the contents of this book. Dean Samira McCarthy, President Benjamin Fiore S.J., Chaplains Theresa Cullen and Stephanie Molloy, and other faculty and staff, espe-cially Joanne Kozlowksi, Chris Riegel, and Allison Fizzard, made my time at Campion wonderfully warm and stimulating.

This is the second book project I have taken to the University of Alberta Press. The ready welcome, lively interaction, and wonderful expertise of Michael Luski, Cathie Crooks, Peter

Midgley, and Alan Brownoff make the detailed work of
bringing a book into print a pleasure rather than a chore,
and the careful copyediting of Meaghan Craven has ensured
that it is as readable as possible. I am grateful for the support
of the Canada Research Chairs Program during the writing
of this book and also of the Aid to Scholarly Publications
Program for a grant in support of printing it.

※ *In Bed with the Word*

ONE

Reading

ON HIS SECOND DAY OF SCHOOL, a boy
has decided to stay in bed with the Word.
He's six years old, and he's in a bunk bed that
has an angle-iron frame and large bolts that
fasten the top and bottom bunks together.
The boy's blonde brush cut is the white fuzz
of a peach circling the dome of his head.
He is nestled in his blankets on the bottom
bunk. A pillow is propped up behind him to
cushion his back against the iron bars of the
bed frame. Morning light from the window

& Longing

to his right falls across the blankets on his lap
and illuminates the pages of a black, leather-
bound King James Bible that's laying open
on the blankets. It is a book he cannot read
yet—in fact, he cannot read any book yet,
for this is only his second day at school.

The room smells of sweaty socks and floor
polish. The bunk above the boy is neatly
made, and its bedspread hangs about a foot
above his head. There are ten other bunks in
the room. They are all neatly made up, and

they are all empty. Usually the room would be loud with the shrill voices of the twenty six- and seven-year-old boys who sleep in these bunks at night, but right now the room is vacant, except for the little boy with the King James upside down on his lap.

"What are you doing in bed, Johnny?" asks a woman's voice. "You should be in school with the other boys."

"Oh," says the tow-headed boy calmly. "I just thought I'd spend the day in bed with the Word."

This story is legendary among those my family tells to remind us of who we are and how we are connected to each other. The boy in the bed is my older brother, John, and the scene took place at Bingham Academy, a boarding school for missionaries' children in Addis Ababa, Ethiopia, where all of the children in my family got our early education. John's dorm mother, Val Neuman, later told my parents how she had gone down the hall to inspect the first graders' room after the boys had finished breakfast and left for their classroom. Apparently, the idea that you had to go to school *every* day had not yet occurred to my six-year-old brother. He had already joined the boys and girls in Miss Macdonald's classroom the day before, and so, having discharged his duty, he had decided after breakfast on the morning of the second day to get back out of his clothes, put on his pyjamas, and spend the day in bed with the Word.

This story is perfect. It provides a perfect picture of my brother: his sincerity of heart, his unaffected and natural piety, and his bent for what our family called "quiet time." He had these qualities at the age of six, and he still has them. It also provides a perfect picture of the centrality of reading to the spiritual life as I know it. What is it that would

have made a boy who hasn't been in school long enough to
know how to read yet, a boy who has been separated from
his parents at much too young an age and who has been
placed in the frightening loud environment of a dormitory, a boy who's too new at the culture of schooling to know
that you don't get to pick and choose when you will and
when you won't go to school—what is it that would make
such a bewildered boy take to his bed with the Word?

There are many reasons. Six-year-old Johnny would have
been looking for comfort, for something familiar, for something that would help him regain his ground, a sense of his
own solidity in his new environment. To do this, he took off
his clothes after breakfast, put on his pyjamas, and got back in
bed among the blankets, sheets, and pillow that Mom had sent
from home. By getting back into bed with the Word, he was
revisiting an early-morning pattern he had witnessed in our
home since the day he was born. Every morning, my mother
and father, for as long as I have known them, have gotten out
of bed, put on the kettle for a hot drink, and picked up their
Bibles and notebooks for what they called quiet time. They
were enacting a version of the ancient practice of *lectio divina*, or
spiritual reading, outlined by the twelfth-century Carthusian
Guigo II, with its four stages of *lectio* (reading), *meditatio* (meditation), *oratio* (prayer), and *contemplatio* (contemplation). Given
their evangelical Protestant tradition, however, my parents
did not use these medieval Latin terms for their practice. They
spent an hour every morning, before the family got up and
started rattling around the house, attending to the Word.

A steaming cup of coffee in your hand and an open Bible on
your lap signified important things in my family. It meant that
you were talking with God and that nobody should interrupt

5

you until the conversation was done. It meant you could smile at each other, even cuddle in beside Mom or Dad on the living room couch, but that you allowed each other solitude so that God's voice would not get drowned out at the start of the day.

I know it sounds a bit rigid for little kids, but I liked this morning quiet time. It meant, not only that I couldn't bug Mom and Dad, but also that they couldn't bug me—not yet. Quiet time meant that we gave each other these respectful moments so we could each settle into our own skins and hearts enough to hear whatever God might have to say. Quiet time enabled a paradox: it created a protected, private place in which you opened yourself vulnerably to God's voice. At one and the same time, you were by yourself and also in intimate communion with an Other—with God. And the way to organize this time, the way to make sure you did listen to God's voice and not just daydream or goof off, was to have an open Bible on your lap. The book on your lap provided focus and structure so that the quiet time wasn't just a blank daze or a wandering mind. The Bible was called the Word, Mom and Dad had taught us, because it was God's voice. You could read it and hear what God had to say right in our own living room, morning after morning, regular as clockwork.

This is the rich vein Johnny was mining that morning when he stayed in bed—the only square inch of privacy a person could find in a dormitory—with the Bible open on his lap. A dormitory can be a shrill, boisterous place. Sharing a room with twenty other six- and seven-year-old boys, each anxious to assert himself in the pack, can be a frightening prospect. For a little boy who is friendly, but who is a little bit shy, spending a morning in bed with the Word would have been a way to withdraw and reconnect. Johnny, therefore, stepped back from the fascinating crowd of boys and girls in his grade one class with their piercing voices and wriggling bodies and tried to reclaim a connection to his family far away, to reach toward the intimacy with God that had been the focus of those warm, quiet mornings with his mother and father, and to pull it around him like the nest of sheets and blankets he had made on his bunk bed in the dormitory. The crucial object that he needed to create this nest was a black, leather-bound King James Version of the Bible.

THE BOY IN BED WITH THE WORD presents in one picture pretty much everything I want to say in this book about spirituality and reading. This story illustrates how reading plunges us into the central paradox of spiritual life, at one and the same time emphasizing and even enforcing our isolation, the fact that we are uniquely and finally alone, while also reminding us that we are connected to and interdependent with the world beyond our own skins, with others, and ultimately with the Other, with God. The boy's loneliness produces a longing, and the book on his lap provides a focus or vehicle for that longing. As well, because he does not yet know how to read, his sitting in bed with the Word gestures toward something before or alongside the meaning-making process of reading itself. Whereas many of us will naturally think of the words on the page and the messages we derive from them as fundamental to the act of reading, before the practice of reading comes the posture of the reader. This picture of the boy indicates how a whole culture of reading surrounds the act itself. The boy doesn't know how to read yet; in fact, he skips a day of classes when he's supposed to be learning how to read because he wants the posture, the position, the place of being a reader. He wants to have the book on his lap and, by so doing, to make contact with his family who are far away. Connection with them is all of a piece with connection to God and to a sense of belonging in the world. The book on his lap is simultaneously a sign of his beloved ones' absence and of his connection to them; it's his way of bridging the distance and bringing them close.

What is it that makes reading, this open book on the lap, such a central posture of the spiritual life? Have you ever wondered about the bookishness of religion—not just Christianity, but most of the world's major religions, including Judaism, Islam, Buddhism, and Hinduism? Why are so many religious folks "People of the Book," to borrow a loaded phrase from the Koran (Muhammed, *Surah* 2:85–121; *Surah* 3:110–15). Why is it that when people want to pray, to worship, to reconnect with their spirits, more often than not, they open a book? Obviously, plenty of people in the world have developed sophisticated spiritual traditions without being literate, so there's no absolute or necessary connection between the reading and writing of books and the capacity for spiritual life. And, there are other forms of expression that are very closely associated with prayer and worship—especially various art forms such as music, painting, sculpture, and architecture. But over and over again, we find that when we strip away the stained glass, incense, prayer beads, or gilded domes of religious expression and peel it down to its basic core, we will find an open book. Why? What is it about reading that is so conducive to spiritual life? What does reading do? What kind of experience does it make that so many people have found it to be fundamental to spiritual awareness?

By *spirituality*, I mean something that clearly flows through our religious impulses and experiences, but it is not identical with them, for it also flows through our psychology and physical sensibility, as well as through our social and political lives. By spirituality, I mean a drive or energy in ourselves that is outward-reaching, that is a kind of longing to be meaningfully connected. I mean what finally moves us, what propels our actions and sparks our imaginations. I mean a recognition of ourselves as connected to others, to the surrounding world, and—within or beyond the sensory world—to the Creator. Spirituality, in this sense, is both generative and responsive: our inner longing drives us outward, but that inner longing rises out of our givenness, our createdness, our dependence on others, on the world, on God. In defining spirituality in this way, I follow the Oblate theologian Ronald Rolheiser, who suggests that spirituality is the shape or structure we give to this basic human longing or energy (Rolheiser 6–7). In this sense, spirituality involves, first, a recognition of our own individuality—how our unique combination of genes, family upbringing, and social setting, with both their blessings and scars, have made us who we are. It then involves a process by which we try to align that unique individuality, find a meaningful place for it, in the movements of the larger social and created order. This understanding of spirituality makes it not just an inner feeling or a psychic state, nor is it merely inner work or the process of interior discernment. It involves these things, but it also requires outward attentiveness to the directions and movements of the world beyond our own minds and hearts. Thus, spirituality is the way we live out our relationships with our environment and with other people, as well as with our secret selves.

The little boy in the bunk bed knew that the book on his lap would channel his longing toward his family and toward

God. The book would give him something productive to do with the welter of emotions inside him—his fear of being abandoned by his parents and his determination to trust their promise to come and see him soon, his attraction to and uncertainty about the children he was meeting in his new school, his anxiety about being in a classroom and what it would be like to learn to read. All these emotions needed somewhere to go, some vessel or channel to drain them off before he burst. He had seen our parents take their anxieties and cares into the quietness of the Word, and he had seen how they emerged from this practice with calm voices and hands that rested gently on his head. So he went where he had seen them go.

A COUPLE OF YEARS EARLIER, on the other side of the world, in the fishing village of Guayguayare, Trinidad, an eight-year-old girl also took to her bed with a book. She had not actually planned on reading; in fact, she had been on the prowl for something sweet. She had watched her grandmother hide foods that would tempt a child—sugar, rum cakes, syrup shine breads, wafers, shortbread—in the bottom drawer of the mahogany wardrobe, under the good tablecloth, good linens, and good pillowcases. She had taken note, through the corners of her eyes, as her grandmother secreted the cakes and cookies under the linens, wiggled the drawer past the spots where it sometimes got stuck, carefully locked it shut, and slipped the key into her bosom. One day, while her grandmother was out, the young girl found a way into the mahogany treasure trove. And it was there, just when she was closing in on sweetness, that she first fell into the face of a book "like a fish falling into water" (Brand 182).

Instead of palming sugar into her pockets, or stuffing rum cakes into her mouth, she became distracted by *The Black Napoleon,* a book on the 1791 Haitian Revolution, which she found in the drawer. The front cover had been torn off, the sepia pages, swollen with the humidity of rainy season, had been traversed by weevils and mapped by silverfish, and the unravelled binding was crusted with dry, amber glue. Syrup cakes forgotten, she leaned over the edge of the drawer and fell into this sea of words. But she soon felt too exposed there, kneeling in front of the wardrobe, so she took the book to her spot behind the house and later, like the boy in the dormitory, to her hiding place under her bed. "This book filled me with sadness and courage," writes Dionne Brand, in *Map to the Door of No Return: Notes to Belonging,* a book that blends personal memoir with large-scale meditation on the scarred history of New World Africans.

> *It burned my skin. I lay asleep on its open face under the bed.*
> *It was the book that took me away from the world, from the*
> *small intrigues of sugar and milk to the pleasure and desola-*
> *tion of words on a page…I had never met Toussaint L'Ouverture*
> *until I saw him at the bottom of the wardrobe drawer with the*
> *cakes and sugar. Perhaps I also met there things I had never*
> *felt before. I did not know about slavery…I did not yet know*
> *how the world took people like me. I did not know history.*
> *The book was a mirror and an ocean…I was eight or so. It*
> *was the first 'big' book I read to its end. When I was finished,*
> *I was made. I had lost innocence and acquired knowledge. I*
> *had lost the idea that desire was plain. (Brand 186–87)*

Again the child takes the book to bed, again it provides a channel for longing, and again it simultaneously isolates her and opens her to a world larger than herself. What starts out as a private quest for sweets plunges her into cultural politics. By this phrase, I don't mean the little "p" of party politics, with its democrats and republicans, Whigs and Tories, communists, socialists, and rhinoceroses. This young Trinidadian girl is plunged into big "C," big "P" Cultural Politics, into a trans-atlantic narrative of vast collective pain and massive, complex yearning that spans generations, into an everyday negotiation of the possibilities and inequities of the world: of who gets to be heard and who doesn't, of who gets some bread and who doesn't, of who gets to love and who doesn't, and who gets to read and who doesn't. What begins for the girl in the small intrigues of a sweet tooth and the possibility of outwitting her grandmother, expands into a mirror and an ocean, a new picture of herself embedded in a long and tortuous history, plus a love for L'Ouverture, the architect of the modern world's first anti-colonial revolution. Finding *The Black Napoleon* in the drawer that smelled of cane sugar and rum, she says, made her the girl who grew up to participate in the Grenadan revolution, to win the Canadian Governor General's award for poetry, and to write books that, in their own turn, burn the skin and wake readers to the world they had not known they inhabited.

But she didn't know these things were in the road ahead when she was eight years old. All she knew then, as she pored over the pages under her bed, was that desire became unplain: what she had thought she wanted, a simple gratification, had opened into something else, a deep lifelong passion. This is what reading can do. "Books leave gestures in the body," Brand writes (191). And this book in the bottom of her grand-

mother's drawer took her out of the world she thought she
had known and cast her into the Black Atlantic, into the trau-
matic story of slavery, a story she had not realized was her
own. She found herself swimming in the tremendous and
overwhelming narrative of African dislocation that has been
reproduced, repeated, resisted, rejected, and then reproduced again throughout the last three hundred years.

The boy in bed with the Word longs for contact with his
absent family; the girl in search of sweets is introduced to the
politics of culture. Both experience the pleasure and desolation
of words on a page. Both experience the book as the focus, the
spark, the channel for longing. Both show that reading occurs
in private but that it doesn't stay there. Instead, reading pushes
the reader beyond the starting point of his or her own mind
and into the larger world. "Why does someone enclose a set of
apprehensions within a book?" Brand asks. "Why does someone
else open that book if not because of the act of wanting to
be wanted, to be understood, to be seen, to be loved?" (192).
Reading exercises and gives shape to the outward-reaching
energy within us that is our spirituality. In this sense, reading
is erotic and like all eros, it leaps with energy and passion;
it compels your focus; it reaches out toward an Other.

"AT THE HEART OF THE PLEASURE OF READING,"
wrote Virginia Woolf, "is the delight in a free union, like a very
intimate conversation or an act of love" (qtd. in Malone 125).

I agree with Woolf, but I have opened this meditation with
two scenes of pre-pubescent child readers to emphasize that the
erotics of reading is not limited to the erogenous zones of adult,
genital sex. The boy and girl both take their books to their beds,
the place of comfort and intimacy, and there they are projected

or lifted out of their immediate worlds. Their desires and long-
ings reach out. They span the gap of solitude and connect to
family, to the world whose shape and contours they are just
coming to recognize, to a dim realization of their place in that
world. The experience is enormous. The book in their bed is
like a dream or a nightmare. It provides the signs and shapes
for impulses and fears they had, of predispositions that were
within them, but of which they were not fully aware. It comes
to them in the middle of things, in the boy's trouble and in
the girl's restlessness, and it becomes a mirror and an ocean.

I associate this experience with erotic longing to emphasize its raw and amorphous energy. As Brand and Woolf both
suggest, the desire to read can become love—whether *agape,
caritas, philia,* or *eros*—but in the first instance it is simply
outward-reaching energy. What is important about it is that,
even in this primal and unexalted state, it flies in the face of
solipsism, the myth of autonomy and self-completeness. The
desire to read emphasizes a basic generosity toward the Other
that is the condition of all language. As Donald Davidson has
argued, entering into language involves us in what he calls
the "principle of charity," an assumption that other people
are intelligible and that they have something worthwhile to
say. We are willing to attend to them, we interact with them,
based on this assumption. Reading emphasizes, even more
than speech, our role in this generous principle because it takes
place in the absence of the writer. The reader is not under the
various subtle pressures to respond politely that are basic to
everyday face-to-face conversation. So, in this sense, she takes
on a greater role than the conversationalist in generating an
interest in the statements of other people. The impulse to read,
therefore, insists on the necessity of the Other—on our need

for, fascination with, surprise by, dependence on others—even in moments of the most intense privacy and self-attention.

Many writers, going right back to Aristotle and St. Augustine, agree with Davidson that reading is based on the principle of charity, although they differ on what name to give to that love. Alan Jacobs follows Augustine in insisting that the outward-reaching energy involved in reading ought to be organized by *caritas*, rightly ordered love for God, others, and oneself, while Wayne Booth, following Aristotle, suggests that it should be more like *philia*, or friendship. There is much to recommend both of these refinements, but I think they are second-order prescriptions for what reading *ought* to be like rather than first-order descriptions of its basic condition. If anything, reading starts with *eros* in its general and unidealized outward-reaching energy, and, like all eroticism, it can vitalize, but it can also burn. It can be imperialistic, consuming all it encounters into its own insatiable appetite, but it can also go out to the Other, open itself to the difference of the Other, become newly self-aware by its intimate contact with that Other.

The erotic element of reading abides in this powerful blurring of inside and outside, this astonishing experience of profound intimacy with another, but it occurs completely in the mind of the reader. "The extraordinary fact in the case of a book is the falling away of the barriers between you and it. You are inside it; it is inside you; there is no longer either outside or inside," writes Georges Poulet. He goes on to a wonderful meditation on the ecstatic fusion that occurs when we read:

> *I am thinking the thoughts of another. Of course, there would be*
> *no cause for astonishment if I were thinking it as the thought of*

another. But I think it as my very own. Ordinarily there is the I
which thinks, which recognizes itself (when it takes its bearings)
in thoughts which may have come from elsewhere but which it
takes upon itself as its own in the moment it thinks them...
Now, in the present case things are quite different. Because of the
strange invasion of my person by the thoughts of another...
I am the subject of thoughts other than my own...Reading,
then, is the act in which the subjective principle which I call I, is
modified in such a way that I no longer have the right, strictly
speaking, to consider it as my I. I am on loan to another, and this
other thinks, feels, suffers, and acts within me. (Poulet 42–45)

The subjective principle that I call "I," is modified. This experience of fusion, of being inhabited by another, of being on loan
to the other, like all erotic experience, is startling and profound,
because it is one of the ways in which we can be set free from
the confines of our own mental and social perceptions and
opened to the perceptions and experiences of others. But that
experience of fusion with the Other can also be dangerous.

I call attention to the danger because I don't want this book
to come across as a "romance of reading." I have no interest
in promoting the idealized image of the reader, alone in his
bower of bliss, sailing splendidly above the sordid world on
a sea of perfect thoughts and beautiful dreams. I do not want
to imply that reading is completely terrific or inherently salv-
ific. There are people who have been damaged by what they
read. Sometimes the fusion of selves becomes a confusion of
selves, so that readers lose track of their actual lives. And sometimes readers have been damaged by the same books that have
been healing for other people. That same black, leather-bound
King James Bible that gave my brother such comfort has been

the cause of many women's self-belittlement and suppression. I have seen women taught by it that God likes men better than them or that there's something in their nature that means they are supposed to stand second in line. That same book has been read over the burning of midwives accused of witchcraft, the lynching of Black men and homosexuals, and the imprisonment of First Nations children in residential schools. And I'm still talking about "the Good Book"; I haven't even gotten to the books of explicit sadism or hatred or prejudice. So, there is no point in being naïve about reading. There can be many effects of reading, and not all of them are for the good.

But the point I want to make here, at the start of this book, is that, in the very basic structure of reading, in the initial situation where a reader enters into a page, we have the core of an impulse that is fundamental and helpful to spiritual life and to cultural politics. As the boy in bed with the Word and the girl under her bed with the book indicate, the urge to read is paradoxical in that the reader withdraws from others not to be shut up in his or her own mind but to connect, intimately, with others, with the larger world, and, potentially, with God. The withdrawal underlines the importance of privacy, intimacy, and self-awareness if we wish to attend meaningfully and imaginatively to the world beyond our own immediate skins. This intimate openness to the Other is vulnerable and tender: the longing of the six- and eight-year-old readers could be easily abused or aborted; it could be turned in hurtful and limiting directions. But in the very existence of this vulnerable longing, there is the potential for everything: for growth, for learning, for love, for self-knowledge and other-knowledge, and especially, for learning to listen to the voice of the Other.

TWO

Reading as

WE LIVE IN THE MIDST of a transition from print culture to screen culture, and, while it is too early to tell what all the effects are going to be, there are spiritual demeanours, habits of mind and heart, developed in print culture that will be increasingly important to us in a culture increasingly dominated by the screen. This fact was driven home for me through two conversations I had with students in the past few years. Both were students in my classes at McMaster University, and, although these two conversa-

Counterculture

tions were absolutely different from each other in tone and direction, they both emphasized for me the importance of a renewed attention to the spiritual dimensions of reading.

The first was a running conversation—it was more like a running debate—that I had with a student in a class I was teaching on modern critical theory. William had spiky blonde hair that was gelled at the tips and blue eyes that flashed intelligent fire as each day he dug in to the delicious game of bait-the-professor.

"I'm a Nietzschean!" he announced early on in the semester. "I read with a will-to-power. I refuse to believe what I'm told. I don't have to accept the politically correct drivel that goes for learning these days—you know, the boatload of crap that everybody's created equal and that the canon of great authors are really just a tottering bunch of White guys held in place by another bunch of White critic-guys." William punctuated each staccato phrase by jabbing an index finger at the top of his desk. "All I have to do is read Shakespeare or Dostoevsky or Hegel, and I can see that even the best of the new writers—the postmoderns and women and post-colonials and Aboriginals—aren't in the same league...."

Any gap in my professorial drone and William's clipped consonants would spatter from his lips—punchy, intelligent, stiletto-sharp. It was this way every single day. For him, each class was an opportunity for a one-on-one debate with me over the heads of his fellow students. I felt bruised and flat-footed by the end of every one. I simply couldn't think quickly enough to keep up with his mad genius, and the more he talked, the more I grew clumsy with frustration and embarrassment. One day at the end of class, I was dusting down the chalkboards, aware that as usual William the Conqueror was waiting for the rest of the class to file out of the room so he could come to the front and close in for a final kill. I was already dead. I was sweeping my own words into the dust tray at the bottom of the chalkboard, and I had no living brain cells left. The fluorescent tubes above me buzzed, loud as the ringing in my ears.

I gradually realized that William was talking, but I hadn't heard him over the traffic in my ears: "...that's why being required to read second-rate stuff—whether it's minority writers or over-hyped theorists—reduces us to become second-rate thinkers ourselves. I'm with Matthew Arnold and Harold Bloom. We should be reading only the best of what's been thought and written in civilized culture."

My hand paused at the bottom of its downward sweep with the chalk duster, and, exhausted, I half-turned toward my interlocutor. "So let me ask you this question, William: why do you read? Why does it matter?"

"I read to enter the great debates." William stabbed the pile of student papers on my desk with his ever-active finger. "I read to transcend the limits of my environment. I read to connect with the greatest minds in history, to see through the superficial and the sloppy thinking in the world around me." He registered each declaration with another jab at the papers. "I read with a will-to-power. I read not to be a slave."

And then he stopped. His sudden silence surprised me, and I turned fully toward him, the chalk duster still in my hand. "You know," he said. "I'm in my fourth year of an honour's degree in English and Philosophy, and nobody has ever asked me that question before. Isn't that a crime? Every single class I take starts and ends with a list of readings upon which we're examined and poked and prodded from September to April, but no one has ever asked why we do it! It's one more example of the sloppiness that passes for education these days. We're made to read what some people pass off as 'critical theory'"—he wiggled two fingers in the air for scare quotes—"but we never ask the basic, crucial questions!"

⁙ THE SECOND CONVERSATION was much more pleasant, compared to William's professor-baiting, so it surprises me that it has lingered in my mind and troubled me just as much. This exchange took place in my office with a soft-spoken and thoughtful graduate student named Annette. She was just finishing the first year of her PhD, and she had come to my office to discuss what she wanted to do now that she was done the coursework part of her studies and could launch into her independent dissertation research.

"I don't *do* literature anymore," she said, as the afternoon sunlight slanted through the Venetian blinds and warmed a rectangular patch on the area rug between her chair and mine. "I've really enjoyed the classes I've been taking this year in Cultural Studies—you know, looking at the power that advertising, television, film, and other popular media like magazines have in our culture. I just can't see myself sitting around in a corner reading poems anymore. Our society is changing so fast, and reading just doesn't have the kind of social impact it used to have—I mean reading traditional texts, like the great authors."

The Department of English, where I teach at McMaster University, was then in a period of transition, and I was very aware that this conversation with Annette was a symptom of that transition. We had introduced a new undergraduate program in Cultural Studies and Critical Theory the year before and were now launching a new master's degree along the same lines. Some of my colleagues were still licking wounds after a difficult meeting in which we had, after impassioned debate, decided to change our name from the "Department of English" to the "Department of English and Cultural Studies."

Annette was not the kind to throw gasoline on the fiery debates we'd had in the department. She was shy and thoughtful, looking past me and out my window toward the maple that was just leafing out beside University Hall. Our department transition was giving her the chance to think carefully about what she should devote her coming years to. "You know that theory of Benedict Anderson's," she continued, "that the modern nation became possible only after the invention of the printing press, because people who had never met one another could now read the same newspaper or novel and therefore imagine themselves as part of the same community? Well, it seems to me that things have changed with new technology. All you have to do is look at the last number of elections and you quickly realize that television and other forms of mass media replaced print literacy and reading a long time ago as the social glue of Western culture. I'm not saying it's good glue, but more and more, it's truly what people share in common."

She's right, I thought. You can start a conversation with pretty much anybody about what movie they've seen recently, but it's hit or miss if you want to connect with someone over a book.

Annette shifted forward in her chair and her green eyes came to rest on my face. "That's what I want to study. I'm fascinated by the new social patterns that are arising from the new technologies. I don't want to do an irrelevant degree. You know, some reading of the images of birds in Chaucer or of the theme of liberty in Faulkner. I don't want to produce pages and pages of soulful musings that rot away on a library shelf somewhere.

"I was looking at the website for the National Institute on Media and the Family in the States," she added, tucking her auburn hair behind one ear. "And it says American children spend more time watching television than anything else but sleeping. Kids between ages two and seventeen watch about twenty-five hours a week! And 56 per cent of American teenagers have TVs in their bedrooms. Pretty amazing, eh? With stats like that, I feel it's important to understand the new world that's emerging these days. Because there are huge problems with the way new media—not just TV, but Internet, and other things like video games—are tied into commodity markets that look free but aren't."

○ MY CONVERSATIONS with William and Annette planted the seeds for this book, because they made me ask myself the question I had asked William: why do I read? What is it about reading that is important, not just for university students but for people in general? What is it in me that flinched during both conversations—especially since they were from opposite sides of the spectrum, with William arguing passionately for a return to the "Great Tradition" of classics and Annette deciding that mass media, not literary classics, should be the objects of study?

Thinking back, I realize that these two conversations troubled me because they both assumed, and therefore overlooked, the remarkable value there is in the deceptively simple-seeming practice of being able to hear a voice and envision a world through printed text. Both conversations overlooked and dismissed vital processes represented by the boy in bed with the Word or the girl falling into the face of *The Black Napoleon*. They ignored the importance of reading as quiet time, as a form of sociable solitude, as a unique experience of intimate projection into the secret world of the Other, as private and politically relevant contemplation. They did not recognize that—far from being irrelevant to a culture that is terrorized (I use the word advisedly) by the results of its own over-consumption—this quiet time is more urgently needed than ever.

These two conversations pushed me beyond the description of what reading is to the more prescriptive topic of what it might or ought to be. Although William was arguing for

what looked like traditional book reading, his approach
disturbed me because, for him, reading was a process of
imperialistic acquisition: he wanted to conquer the books
of the greatest writers he could find. The "great" books he
read would become building blocks in the fortifications he
wanted to erect between himself and the world whose shab-
biness offended him. For him, the greater the books, the
stronger the defense. Annette, by contrast, held no such elitist
views. She wanted to read the very commonplace texts that
repulsed William. She had little interest in the "greats," saw
their elevated contents as so far removed from where everyday
people live as to be irrelevant. She wanted to turn her attention to the new media forms that are replacing the world
of print as our society's social glue. For her, critical study of
these new texts was a way to engage with the world as it is, to
concentrate on real social problems that need to be addressed.
I admired her desire for relevance, but I felt that something
would go missing—something crucial and relevant—if
reading were taken for granted. She would need a value derived
from reading, I thought, in order to bring a critical perspec-
tive to the popular media forms she wished to critique.

   Although the conversations with William and Annette may
look like they are about the choices of what to read, the more
I have thought about this, the more I have come to think the
choice of reading material is an important, but a secondary,
concern. I agree with St. Augustine, who saw that even what
was for him the holiest of books, the Scriptures, is a vehicle
for the journey rather than its destination. For Augustine,
loving the Bible for itself was a form of idolatry; we are to
use the Scriptures to build charity, to be led out of ourselves
and into dialogue with the Other, with God, not to fall in

love with the book itself. Following Augustine, I have come
to believe that reading is important because of what reading
does, because of how it positions us in relation to the world
around us, to others—to the Other. That is, it is important
because it fosters a spirituality—not the only spirituality, or
even the most important kind of spirituality—but a spirituality that is increasingly, as Annette's comments implied,
counter-cultural. Reading is counter-cultural mainly because
it requires quiet time, being slow and meditative, and it is
active rather than passive, being imaginative and dialogical. These qualities run in the opposite direction from the
one in which Western commodity culture is heading.

The conversion of thoughtful citizens into impatient
consumers requires that we live in constant distraction, that
our restlessness be fuelled by a sense of present dissatisfaction
and endlessly deferred fulfillment. This restlessness is made
to saturate every nook and cranny of our lives. It's hard to keep
your eyes on the traffic because huge pixel boards flash images
of fast cars and beautiful women as you drive down the street;
you clear your letter box of dozens of leaflets, screen incoming
phone calls from telephone solicitors, and delete dozens of
spam messages from your e-mail inbox every few days. This
week, when I swiped my card to pay for gas at the Esso station,
a TV screen leapt to life just above the pump and blared the
attractions of Esso while I, trapped by having to squeeze
the trigger on the pump, was forced to listen. Over and over
again, the language of these advertisements is the language
of hurry. When was the last time you saw an ad that asked you
to take your time and to meditate carefully before choosing a
product? No, we are constantly made to feel that the good life
is a scarce commodity that will pass us by unless we hurry on

down and buy it now. Commodity culture foments the logic of scarcity—there is never enough, the supplies are about to run out, so hurry up and purchase before you lose your chance.

Now, it is easy to lash out at mass media—commercial television, blockbuster films, sponsored computer media, ad-ridden magazines—because they are the primary purveyors of this widespread restlessness and discontent. But there are public television stations, independent films, computer media, and magazines that resist the pressures of the commodity market, so it is important that we not make the mistake of lumping all of these media forms into one guilty category. For one thing, we must admit that some kinds of books are major purveyors of commodification. Think of the mass sales of Harlequin Romances, of self-help books, or of what a friend of mine calls "deco-porn"—the many glossy photo books that feed our lust for renovated kitchens and home accessories. There are kinds of printed texts that operate wholly in the service of commodification, and there are forms of audio-visual media that sharply oppose it.

Nonetheless, it's not hard to see that the highly commercialized culture of the screen appeals to, and works to produce, a very different kind of audience than do less-commerce-driven media and books. Basically, commerce-oriented media are restless and fast. The images of blockbuster films, most TV, and computer media flick across your retina at lightning speeds, each replacing the previous, and in turn being replaced by the next at a rate too fast for the mind to register. This speed creates the feeling that what you are viewing is unmediated, direct experience. In fact, part of the pleasure of these forms is the dizzy feeling of speed itself. The car chases, split-second martial arts moves, sudden explosions, and high-tech special effects of the television and movie industries, pictured on larger and larger screens and through bigger and bigger sound systems, convey powerful sensation and inassimilable speed.

In comparison, reading is low-key and slow. The eye must pass, one word at a time, across the line on the page or on the computer screen in order to create whatever mental images, thoughts, or sensations the reader experiences. Reading requires patience, for you can't know the meaning of what you're reading until you reach the end of the sentence, the end of the page, the end of the book. This very slowness, the effort required to transform printed text into mental sensation, demands a particular kind of person: a quietly active reader. As Elaine Scarry has pointed out, printed text is unique among the various arts, because, unlike painting, photography, music, sculpture, or architecture—let alone multimedia—it contains almost no sensuous content. Painting uses actual colours, textures, and shapes to convey its concepts and impressions to the viewer's mind; music produces sounds you can actually hear; and architecture uses walls you can physically touch and floors you can walk on. By contrast, written text provides extremely meagre sensuous material: a series of black marks on a page or symbols on a computer screen physically unrelated to the mental images these marks seek to convey (Scarry 3–9).

Art forms that provide the most complete set of physical sensations convey an illusory immediacy—that is, they tend to hide their own status as made objects, as media—because they require less imaginative activity from the viewer or listener, whereas sparer forms involve a more active interpreter. Because multimedia forms, such as television and film, provide not just moving visual images but also soundtracks for them, the viewer is told not just what the story looks like but also what

emotions to associate with its images. This is another dimension to the illusion of immediacy that audiovisual media can
create: our emotional responses to the swelling orchestra-
tion, the frenetic drumming, or the tender flute music make
us imagine that we feel these things ourselves. But we were fed
these emotions: almost none of our response was something
we came up with on our own. The director of a movie directs
not only the actors, not just the makers of props and special
effects; he or she also directs the responses of the spectators.

Obviously, the writer of a text, too, attempts to direct the
reader's emotional responses. But the sensuous deprivation
of print, the structure of absence or gap between the signi-
fying system and its intended meanings—whereby marks on
a page or computer screen refer to a sensory world in which
they do not actually participate—means that the writer has
very limited access to the mind of the reader. The reader will
create his or her own mental images and soundtrack from the
marks on the page, and the writer can suggest their quality
but has no say over how the reader will apprehend them.

Again, it's important, as I lay out this discussion, that we
not draw an airtight dichotomy between printed text and
multimedia. For one thing, books often contain illustrations
to supplement the printed text, and for another, many multimedia forms, such as computer games and subtitled films,
rely heavily on printed text. In addition, Scarry notes that
among literary forms, poetry, with its use of sound effects,
such as metre and rhyme, incorporates a heightened sensory
content compared with standard prose (7). We should also
observe that although audiovisual forms, such as films or television, produce actual physical sensations that relate directly
to the ones they wish to evoke in the viewer, they can be slow-

moving and constructed with so many layers of intention and association that they require as much interpretive effort from the audience as a good book does. It is more helpful, then, to think of a continuum of art forms between those that are more and those that are less susceptible to commodification (ones that require more or less mental activity from the audience) than it is to draw a line between books and multimedia.

◌ FOR MY PURPOSES, reading names the interpretive activity that literate cultures developed most consciously in relation to communicating by means of marks on a page, but it is that process of thoughtful interpretation itself, the activity of imaginative understanding, that is of greater value than the marked pages. We must not confuse the vehicle with the destination of the journey. Books are important because their sensory sparseness—their distance from the sensuous worlds to which they refer—can remind us of the astonishing work of the imagination in human communication. But, as Annette pointed out, one can imaginatively and alertly "read" anything—including the home shopping channels of commodity culture—once one has learned the posture and practice of the reader. Reading, then, involves a specific kind of relationship between the medium and its audience. Whereas the consumption of sensory-rich media is fast and passive, reading is slow and active. Readers must do the actual mental and physical labour of tracing the lines of print across the page, across page after page, and to exercise their capacities for recognition, comprehension, and imagination to create meaning from it. If there is speed, such as the urgency to rip through the pages of a mystery novel, this speed is created and enacted by the reader's own ability to read and animate the lines of text as quickly as he or she can. But for the most part, reading is relatively slow, and this slowness offers the reader a countercultural, spiritual exercise.

Reading a passage can help a reader remember the pleasures of reflection, the relief of not being restless and of having time to follow a complete thought that has not been reduced to a sound bite or an advertiser's slogan. And here is where the secondary consideration of what to read enters into the picture, for, to gain these benefits, readers must seek out particular forms of reading that emphasize continuity and slowness. The advantage of a book over a magazine, for example, is that most books don't interrupt the text with advertising; the same is true of a publicly funded television station as opposed to a commercial one, or of a website free of banners or pop-up screens as compared to ones that are rife with flashing, click-me images. In each case, the reader can choose continuity and slowness over interruption and restlessness. Among print forms, for example, poetry, because of its compression, requires readers to read a line over several times. Poetry highlights—through the echo of sounds, parallel structures, forms of contrast, images and metaphors—the multi-layered meanings of any given sentence. Even fiction, which one might imagine is the "fastest" literary form because it tends to build tension and curiosity in the reader, involves layers of characterization, symbol, and social circumstance that require the reader's time and reflection. Art photography or painting, whose images carry allusive power, whose colours, shapes, and textures convey mental states, social analyses, or whole histories, demand careful and sustained attention. Contemplative reading, then, is countercultural for a generation that is increasingly drawn away from silence, slowness, reflection, and internally generated imagination.

Reading is also countercultural because its emphasis on active interpretation over passive consumption produces critically alert rather than naïvely accepting readers. It encourages Annette's desire to engage seriously with contemporary commodity culture. And, although I found William the Conqueror's views harder to appreciate, reading feeds his desire to take on challenging rather than superficial material. Both student conversations remind me of the value of what Paul Ricoeur has called a hermeneutics of suspicion. Ricoeur identifies two poles that define a tension between them in the history of interpretation. He calls the first the hermeneutics of affirmation or faith, and he associates it with the religious belief that revelation has occurred already and that the process of reading or interpretation involves the realization or recollection of that revelation's depth of meaning. Ricoeur calls the second pole the hermeneutics of suspicion and associates it with Nietzsche, Freud, and Marx, each of whom looked upon consciousness as primarily delusional or false. For the hermeneutics of affirmation, the text is to be venerated, appreciated, and analyzed for its truth and beauty; for the hermeneutics of suspicion, the text is unaware of its own motivations or contents, like Freud's unconscious or Marx's lumpenproletariat, and the reader needs to discover what it is that exists behind the text's lack of self-awareness. In the first, there is a great veneration and care for the object one is analyzing, while in the second the object is understood as an illusion or disguise which must be stripped away (Ricoeur 28–30). Ricoeur's point is not to argue for the value of one of these approaches to the exclusion of the other; rather, he insists that they form a tension, an extreme polarity, which is "the truest expression of our 'modernity'" (27).

You can witness the tension in this polarity in the pendulum swings that have occurred in literary criticism during the twentieth century. In the first half of the century, under the dictates of what was called at the time "New Criticism," students were taught to appreciate the subtlety, ingenuity, and perfection of "high" art. More often than not, these works were produced by White, middle- or upper-class European men, and this small sampling's rather narrow view of the world and of what makes great art usually passed under the radar. Readers were not encouraged to think about the cultural contexts that produced the work but to venerate the text itself. Then, with the countercultural movements of the 1960s—Civil Rights, the American Indian Movement, the Women's Movement, Gay and Lesbian Rights, and the widespread decolonization of Europe's former colonies—the arts became politicized in a way they hadn't been in the early part of the century. Literary and cultural critics called attention to the way women's perspectives, working-class experiences, the artistic work of Black or Indigenous creators, and the remarkable number of homosexual artists all went unacknowledged in what people thought of as the "Great Tradition."

This political awakening occurred in the middle of my own training in graduate school, and it brought a whole new impetus to my studies. Suddenly, the skills I had been developing for reading, for slow meditation upon multi-layered and richly allusive writing, were given a new burst of energy. Reading was no longer merely a self-improving, inward activity. I became aware of its social and political dimensions. My reading and my writing about my reading could participate in wider movements for social justice. I came to see that what

I read *did* matter, not because of criteria such as "high" and "low" art, but because reading, and writing about what I read, could bring other voices—often long-neglected or suppressed voices—not just to my own attention but also onto the public stage and into the public ear. I became alert to the politics of literature and culture. I learned, and in turn I began to teach my students, the hermeneutics of suspicion—how to read novels, plays, poems, television shows, films, magazines, or shopping malls to become aware of the consumerist, colonialist, White-supremacist, sexist, homophobic, or upper-class values that produced and are reinforced in these various cultural forms. I came to see that intelligent readers of the late-twentieth and early twenty-first centuries need to be not so much appreciators as critics who suspiciously examine the "text"—whether it's a poem or a billboard—to see how its often unspoken assumptions shape us into "subjects" of our cultural circumstances.

I am grateful for this pendulum swing. If we are to avoid being passive consumers, it is very important that we not be naïve readers who uncritically admire whatever we read. I have taken great delight in seeing how my love for aesthetically rich materials has evolved from a private pleasure into a publicly oriented, politically engaged activity. Over the course of the last thirty years, we have seen not just curricular changes take place at universities but also major shifts in what gets produced, published, and read. Publishers now print highly successful books, major movie companies now produce popular films, and gallery curators exhibit the top-notch works of Indigenous, female, or non-Western artists. In thirty short years, the names of authors such as Salman Rushdie and Louise Erdrich, filmmakers such as Spike Lee and Deepa Mehta, musicians such as Cesária Évora and Ladysmith Black

Mambazo, and architects such as Douglas Cardinal and Dillon Kombumerri have become internationally renowned. What cheers me about these developments isn't so much the success of these individuals but the way their work brings to public attention the worlds from which they come. Awareness of their work makes it harder to believe the high-gloss illusions of commodity culture, makes it harder to ignore the immigrant ghettos of London, the Black underclass of the USA, gays and lesbians not just in the West but in India, the layering of migrant cultures on the Cape Verde islands, as well as in Durban, and the persistence of Indigenous peoples everywhere.

So I celebrate what has been produced by the kinds of reading practices that question the traditional canons. But I also see the recent emphasis on the hermeneutics of suspicion, like many corrective measures, as a pendulum swing that can lose something important when it abandons the hermeneutics of affirmation. That something is humility, which, along with slowness and critical alertness, is another countercultural, spiritual value that can be gained from reading. Commodity culture creates restlessness by means of a contradictory propaganda that aims to convince us simultaneously of our entitlement and our inadequacy. We are bombarded with messages that insist we deserve the best—car, underarm deodorant, diamond necklace, or mouthwash—but we do not have them yet. We will not be happy until we do. The remarkable thing about the simplicity of this contradictory propaganda is that, despite our better judgement, it works. People *know* advertising is aimed at the production of restlessness, but we still go out and buy the over-praised product. No wonder our situation calls for a posture of perpetual suspicion. We are accustomed to being manipulated by messages in which we place little or no credence. We are used to seeing through the banality and hype that nonetheless seduces us. We are used to living in irony.

My conversations with William and Annette outline two of the most common responses to this ironic situation. William's response was to try to escape it, to insist that he could simply sail above his shabby culture by shutting out the world and associating only with the enlightened elite. The problem here is that the cynicism of commodity culture had already contaminated his method. The greatest books of the greatest writers were not, for him, guides or doorways into the complex world. They were not mentors he could open himself to and receive wisdom from. They were territories he wished to conquer, sparring partners that he hoped to best. He believed his intelligence entitled him to their thoughts, and, by engaging with them, he aimed to build from their brilliant ideas and immense learning a lofty eminence that would set him apart from the sloppy thinking and squalor around him. Despite his argument for the Great Tradition, the texts of that tradition were commodities he wished to acquire, and he approached them from the unself-questioning position of one who approaches all things from a hermeneutics of suspicion.

By contrast, Annette wanted to engage mass culture on its own terms. I respected her approach more than William's because it started from a position of humility. She didn't see herself as superior to her neighbours. She saw herself as subject to the illusions of our culture, not sailing high above them, and she wanted to try to understand their power. In this sense, she was like the three masters of suspicion, Nietszche, Freud, and Marx, who Ricoeur says carried Cartesian doubt right into its stronghold since they were willing to doubt consciousness itself and thereby to liberate and extend it (33–34). Likewise,

Annette wanted to learn, to try to understand where our culture
is taking us, and she was willing to examine the vehicles and
strategies of commodity culture in which she herself was
embedded to try to gain this understanding. Hers was a less
combative approach than William's, but it was just as much one
of suspicion because it chose objects for study that it could not
trust or appreciate. In both cases, a hermeneutics of affirmation went missing. An interpretive practice that can approach
a work—a poem, novel, painting, piece of music, film, or TV
show—with a sense of awe and admiration was absent. This
is significant because without an experience of awe or admiration, reading has very little chance of changing the reader.

⬚ IT DOES MATTER WHAT WE READ, therefore, not
because an authority of some kind has told us a certain work
must be respected above all others and we should genu-
flect before it, but because it is impossible to adopt a posture
of openness and vulnerability before a text we despise, or
one we fear or distrust. As people are increasingly subjected
to commodity culture, we are used to closing ourselves to
messages all around us. When the TV screen started blaring
its wares at the Esso station, I stared hard at the pump handle
and refused to look up. They can force their sounds into my
ears, I thought, but they can't make me watch their images.

We get so used to this self-hardening, whether in response
to telephone solicitors at mealtimes or puppies and babies on
TV, that we begin to think this defensive posture is natural.
Under such conditions, reading a thing that is truly admir-
able, whether it is on a page, a canvas, celluloid film, or a plasma
screen, comes as a bit of a shock, because it reminds us what
it is like to be open and undefended. We need this reminder,

not just because it can be a private pleasure, but because of the way it opens us to the Other. It is difficult to find nourishment or sustenance in texts for which we have little respect, ones that are so single-voiced or formulaic that we know what they are going to say before they say it. If we approach books or films that are unwise, unintelligent, or easily discernable, they can only leave us cold and unmoved, or, worse, conceited about our ability to see through their weaknesses so readily. Such works can only confirm our illusion of superiority. If we are to be challenged by a painting or a poem, to be opened to the voice of the Other in a TV program or an essay, to be expanded beyond our present scope by a photograph or a novel, we need to read texts that are smarter or wiser than we are on our own. We need to read texts that engage with the complex moral and ethical situations we often feel overwhelmed by, ones that open up aspects of human and natural life in the world that we could not possibly understand or perceive without guidance or, at least, wise company. We need to read works that draw out our surprise, call up our admiration, devastate our current assumptions, and call us to a wider experience than we currently have. We need to read works that are bigger than ourselves.

Texts bigger than ourselves call forth an admiration or awe that is a necessary counterbalance to the perpetually egocentric position of unremitting critique, with its assumption that I will always see through the banality of the text at hand. This position is not just one of hubris but also of blindness because it cannot learn, cannot experience awe, and can therefore only tread upon beauty. To put it differently, texts that are larger than ourselves can encourage what Ricoeur calls a "second naïveté," an openness that has undergone criti-

cism, since it admits its own capacity for delusion even as
it trusts in the possibility that the text has something new
and powerful to reveal (28). Spirituality, driven by the need
to connect meaningfully with myself, the world around me,
and to the Otherness of God and humanity, demands more
than a hermeneutics of unmitigated suspicion, for it is prem-
ised on my own creatureliness. As a creature, I am subject
to the as-yet-unexplained larger whole of which I am a tiny
and often blind part. Spirituality assumes that I have something to learn and that I can learn it from many things around
me that draw me out of myself. Nature, art, the physical and
spiritual beauty of other people, as well as their creativity
and wisdom, can draw me out beyond the contained space of
my own perceptions. And so can reading. In fact, as I explain
throughout these chapters, reading can play a vital role in exer-
cising our spirituality. Reading simultaneously isolates us and
requires us to actively bridge the structure of absence between
ourselves and others. It demands that we become people who
digest words slowly and thoughtfully. Because it is slow and
reflective; because it requires an active, rather than a passive,
audience; because it is dialogical, a kind of conversation among
an author, her reader, and other readers; because it can acti-
vate both affirmation and suspicion; and because even the
most straightforward forms of writing call for multiple levels
of interpretation—for all these reasons, reading is spiritual.

I have emphasized here, maybe even over-emphasized,
the importance of a hermeneutics of affirmation because of
the way the hermeneutics of suspicion now predominates
in the academy where I live and work. But I do not mean, by
this emphasis, to denigrate the spiritual necessity of suspicion. Reading is a spiritual exercise that raises the chances of

its practitioners becoming critically aware citizens rather than passive consumers. Reading can produce more people who are part of what a prominent aide to President George W. Bush called the "reality-based community." In an article in the *New York Times,* Ron Suskind illustrates how important the citizen-reader is to a society in which the cynicism of commodity culture has fed into the highest realms of public life. This article reports that in the summer of 2002, a senior advisor to President Bush told Suskind that people like him who did investigative reporting were part of "what we call the reality-based community," which he defined as people "who believe that solutions emerge from your judicious study of discernible reality." Such approaches, the advisor said, were a thing of the past. "That's not the way the world works anymore," he said. "We're an empire now, and when we act, we create our own reality." Like advertising, like the transformation of every single thing in the world into a commodity, the senior advisor asserts that his government will create "reality." And, to some extent, he speaks the truth. Our seduction by the empire of commodities does create realities. Our addiction to independent movement in cars makes us demand an oil-based economy that cannot allow the second largest oil-producing country in the world, Iraq, to remain outside of Western control (even if there is no evidence of weapons of mass destruction, a former "reality," later faded into oblivion). The desire for immediate consumer goods has produced greater credit card debt than ever witnessed before in the United States, and the government of Bush's American empire introduced a larger debt than it had ever previously carried. Massive challenges in knowing what to do with huge volumes of waste are the products of restless over-consumption. And to maintain this very rickety

empire, people's capacity for "judicious study"—that is, the
ability to pay attention—must be ceaselessly leached away by
a society of spectacle and distraction. We have governments
that proudly trumpet their policies of acting *without* judicious
and careful study. These governments are indistinguishable
from the business corporations that bank on a public that will
passively consume their manufactured versions of reality, a
public that cannot (or will not) read beyond the preformulated
surfaces of their propaganda. The policies of these masters
of consumer culture are indeed producing our realities.

Thoughtful, slow, critical, and appreciative reading is
spiritually crucial in times like these. If we are to see beyond
the cynicism of commodity culture, if we are to engage in
the hard work of expanding democracy and producing
citizens instead of consumers, we need to become affirma-
tive and suspicious readers. So it does matter what we read,
but it matters even more who we become by reading.

THREE

Posture

THERE ARE MANY OBJECTIONS to thinking of reading as central to the spiritual life. This fact was emphasized for me by a conversation I had with Bob, our red-bearded Buddhist postman.

I had taken a sabbatical from McMaster University and was living in a little rented house in Edmonton, Alberta, where each day I'd get up, make coffee, have breakfast with my wife, Wendy, have some quiet time of reading and prayer, and then sit down on the striped cotton couch with my notebook computer to work on the book I was completing. Every morning, at about 10:30, Bob would stomp up the little wooden staircase to the letterbox beside the front door, slip in the day's mail, give me a friendly wave, and stride off down the sidewalk. The bounce in his step made me think he must be carrying a tune in his head, though he never wore earphones. One day, when I was signing for a parcel, we got to talking.

"What are you working on every day there on the couch?"
he asked, a friendly light leaping from his blue eyes.

"I'm revising the last chapter of a book on early Canadian
literature. I'm excited because now I can get on to my next
project."

"So you're a writer. What kind of stuff do you write?"

"Mostly scholarly stuff. I'm a professor of Canadian literature. But my next project is going to be on the spirituality
of reading."

"Whoa!" he said, eyes still bright behind his wire-rimmed
glasses. He tugged at the bill of his navy blue Canada Post base-
ball cap. His eyes settled on the mauve lilacs blooming beside
the little wooden staircase. "I used to be a huge reader. Got
going on the novels of Robertson Davies for awhile, which
turned me on to Carl Jung. I loved Jung's way of linking psychology and spiritual life together. Read his stuff for several years,
but not any more."

"Why not?" I asked.

He turned his eyes back to me. "Well, reading can only take
you so far, and then it becomes a kind of ceiling. My spiritual
teacher says if you want to go further, you have to sit in silence.
There's no substitute for sitting. Reading distracts you, makes
you restless for one thought after another. He says the first
thing he has to do with North Americans is break them of their
addiction to books. Reading makes you passive, lets you ride
on someone else's experience rather than exploring your own.
Illiterate people back home in India, he said, go 'Boom!'—right
through to deep insight long before people from the West,
because Westerners' minds are too full of the words and ideas
they've read. They aren't truly present to their own reality."

Plenty of people with long experience in the spiritual life agree with Bob. The fourteenth-century author of the *Cloud of Unknowing* reminds us that we cannot know God in any complete way because God is a being we can only love. Books and reading, he says, can give us elementary knowledge, but love comes through the cloud of unknowing, the experience of God's presence in and beyond the darkness and limitation of the human mind. The seventeenth-century Jesuit Jean-Pierre de Caussade agreed: we don't become wise in the knowledge of God by reading books or doing historical research, he writes to the nuns whom he served as spiritual director. Reading can confuse and inflate the ego when we "stuff our minds out of mere greed" for knowledge, which leaves little room for God to actually speak in the present (de Caussade 67, 79). Thich Nhat Hanh, the Vietnamese monk and twentieth-century peace activist, sums up these views with this advice: "If you talk about things you have [only read about but] not experienced, you are wasting your and other people's time. As you continue the practice of looking deeply, you will see this more clearly, and you will save a lot of paper and publishing enterprises and have more time to enjoy your tea" (Hanh 198).

These giants on the spiritual path agree with Bob. Reading *can* indeed get in the way of growth in the spiritual life, especially when people fall under the illusion that they've already mastered what they've experienced only vicariously in books, or, alternatively, when they turn sacred scriptures into chapter and verse rules and regulations that have very little to do with training one's heart and mind to commune with God, creation, and the unsaid that's always circulating in our daily lives. Every significant spiritual tradition teaches people the importance of silencing the noise in one's life and learning to listen to the less-obvious, less-sensational signs and expressions that are around and within us every day. As the Hebrew prophet Elijah discovered, the voice of God comes, not so much in the drama of thunder, lightning, or windstorm as it does in the still, small voice.

⊙ WHILE I'M ACKNOWLEDGING the objections to reading as an aid to spiritual growth, let me carry on—we might as well address them early on in this book. Another objection is encapsulated in the common-sense ways we dismiss people who always have their "nose in a book." Basically, the idea here is that, for some people, books are not doorways that open into the world in which they live; instead, as in the case of William the Conqueror, reading is a defence or an escape, a wall to keep the world out. We've all met people who read assiduously, and can quote you date and fact and page, but who can't use this knowledge in any productive way except to show they know more than others. We say of such people that it's all "book learnin'" and "he's got his head in the clouds," while his feet are caked in manure. There are many versions of this figure, from the innocent one of the child who drives his mother crazy because he disappears into a book and neglects his household chores, to the significant number of professors I've met who read books all day about the nuances of human relationships but who are terrible at relating to others.

The serious objection, carried within these common-sense criticisms, is that reading is an individual act that can alienate people from the flesh and blood people around them. We have a dramatic reminder of the interiority that can come with reading in the fourth-century autobiography of Augustine, Bishop of Hippo. In the sixth book of his *Confessions,* the North African bishop describes his frustration in trying to start a discussion on theological matters with the popular speaker, Ambrose, Bishop of Milan. Apparently, when Ambrose had done entertaining his many guests each day, he would take a quiet time, reading silently by himself in his cell. Augustine is so struck by this odd behaviour that he takes time to describe it in some detail. "When he read," reports Augustine, "his eyes scanned the page and his heart sought out the meaning, but his voice was silent and his tongue was still" (qtd. in Manguel 42). You see, silent, individual reading had not yet become a common practice, so Augustine had hoped to start a discussion with Ambrose when he sat and listened to Ambrose read aloud. Maybe he could break in at some point and ask Ambrose to make some comments on whatever he was reading. In the fourth century, priests and teachers like Augustine and Ambrose were among the educated elite, and their role was to announce the words they read to their congregations and students. Reading, during this period of transition from oral to literate culture, was a proclamatory activity. If you visited a scriptorium where monks were preparing fair copies of biblical texts or writings of the church fathers, you would hear a holy buzz of muttering as the monks mouthed the words they were copying onto the page. St. Ambrose's voiceless reading frustrated Augustine's hopes of engaging with him over the text, and, in so doing, provided one of the first recorded instances we have of the realization that reading can be an individual, interior activity—something a person can do by him or herself. Scholars have marked this anecdote in Augustine's *Confessions* as a significant step in the rise of the idea of the individual in Western culture.

But this capacity for individual reading raises the problem
I have already hinted at. Because reading can take place inside
an individual person's head, it can create the prideful illusion of private property—that what I've read, I've mastered.
This is the illusion that because I've *understood* the wisdom of
Shakespeare or Shakyamuni Buddha or Black Elk or Jelaluddin
Rumi or Jesus Christ, that it's somehow mine, as if I own it,
a quality that makes me superior to others around me. As if
I thought it up myself. Readers can be insufferable. To adapt
a phrase from the Biblical epistle of James, people who are
hearers only and not doers of the Word are like people who
look at a picture of beauty or virtue and think it's a mirror
of their own attributes. What they read stalls, becoming an
acquisition rather than sparking change or transformation.

Plato famously voiced some strong objections to reading
in the third-century-BC dialogue that he reports between the
teacher Socrates and one of his disciples, Phaedrus. Toward the
end of the dialogue, Socrates tells the following parable. The
god Thoth (or Theuth in some translations) was an inventor
of many ingenious things including arithmetic, geometry,
dice, and astronomy. But his greatest invention was the art
of writing. Thoth came to the King of Egypt and explained
the ways in which these various inventions would benefit
his people. Of writing, he claimed that it would improve
people's memories and make them wiser. The King, however,
objected, arguing that far from aiding memory, writing
would supplant it. Written text is not a recipe for *memory*,
he insisted, but for *reminder*. So, he concluded, "it is no true
wisdom that you offer your disciples, but only its semblance,
for by telling them of many things without teaching them
anything, you will make them seem to know much, while

for the most part they will know nothing. And as men filled
not with wisdom but with the conceit of wisdom, they will
be a burden to their fellow men" (qtd. in Manguel 58).

Socrates's story makes the point that oral culture's
dependence and emphasis on memory—mnemonic tech-
niques, rhetorical rules, oral story forms, refrains, and other
methods for remembering one's cultural inheritance—will
not be aided, but undermined, by literacy. And he's right
insofar as cultural memory will not be retained in people's
minds but rather in the technology or tool of print. Socrates
has anticipated the maxim I was taught in teachers college:
it's not necessary to know everything but to know where
to look it up. Because of this imposition of a mediating
technology between people and what they know, cultural
memory becomes dissociated from the "living memory"
of daily, face-to-face conversation and storytelling.

I remember an Ethiopian friend of mine when we were
small boys who could recite his family's genealogy back ten
generations. We stood in our backyard in the scented shade
of the eucalyptus trees at Obi mission station while Negussie
reeled name after name out of his memory. (It wasn't until
years later that I learned this knowledge was necessary; for
during the negotiations over an Ethiopian marriage proposal,
the relatives check back seven "houses" or generations to
make sure the prospective couple are not related.) He was
shocked to learn that all I could recall was Grandpa Adamson
on my mom's side and Great-grandpa McAlpine on my dad's.
Being from an oral culture, he was taught to remember his
ancestors by name, whereas I, from a literate culture, can
only recall four generations. I don't need to remember all
those names and dates because I can go and look them up

on the family tree my sister once put together. Negussie
knew who his people were; I know them by means of ink on
a page. My ancestors are lying somewhere in a file folder.

If spirituality is about how we shape our longing for connection to others and to the larger world, then you can see how
this shift from living, everyday memory to the one-step-
removed technology of print creates a different spirituality.
In literate culture, knowledge, wisdom, and memory become,
to an extent, abstracted or removed from daily life. Putting
thoughts into print means they can be transported across
great distances, across cultures, even across time and history;
but it also removes them from their organic context. As the
wise King of Egypt foresaw, literacy can displace what we
might call popular, embodied knowledge; it can alienate
you from a sense of intimate connection to others, to what
you collectively know, to what you share in common.

But the Egyptian king objected to writing for
a second reason, one that Socrates elaborates upon, and this
is the inability to control the reader's interpretation. When a
person makes a comment in conversation, Socrates explains,
the listener will reveal by his response whether or not he under-
stands it. And if the speaker sees he's been misunderstood,
he can then rephrase, defend, or explain his point. But when
the exchange takes place by means of a book, the author has
no way to ensure that his statement is properly understood.
Once the words have been written down, Socrates says, "they
are tumbled about anywhere among those who may or may
not understand them, and if they are maltreated or abused,
they have no parent to protect them; and they cannot protect
and defend themselves" (Plato 324). So Socrates's second objec-

tion to reading boils down to an anxiety about control: the technology of print makes orphans of one's words, and they go out into the world with no one to make sure that they are properly understood or protected. At the root, then, Socrates distrusts independent readers, for face-to-face conversation gives the speaker more interactive control over what listeners will make of his words, while the writer is at the mercy of readers. For Socrates, readers have too much liberty.

Now this liberty of the reader is not as completely free as Socrates suggests, for the marks on the page, in their very difference from other marks, define a limit to their possible meanings. If Plato writes that Socrates and Phaedrus are sitting in the shade of a plane tree, it's only a perverse reader who will imagine them sweating and squinting under a blazing sun. The reader needs to imagine what kinds of trees were likely to have grown in ancient Greece and what kind of relief their shade provided under the Mediterranean sun. A good reader has a responsibility to interpret the signs on the page within the conventions understood by the writer—grammar, possible meanings of words as commonly held in the writer's context, how that context sets horizons for the range of possible meanings, and so forth. But to me what's fascinating and delightful about the danger of literacy, like the danger of spiritual life, is precisely that it takes place in a free environment—one not predetermined and absolutely controlled by the author. To come to understand a text, a reader must be free to explore its possible meanings, must freely submit his capacity for interpretation to a reasonable approximation of the possibilities available in the author's context, but in this very submission the reader *projectively animates* the meanings of that text.

This is a point I will return to, for it is fundamental to my understanding of the spiritual benefits of reading, but let us remind ourselves that readers produce the meanings of the text, as the boy and girl who took their books to their beds did, out of longing, out of curiosity, out of an impulse to develop some meaningful connection to experience wider than their own—and in this sense, then, out of something like love. For the reader's projection is responsive, not just egocentric. It is a response, first of all, to the conventions of words themselves, to the meanings readers learned from their linguistic culture that allow them to make any sense of words at all. But it is a response, in the second instance, to the author's initiative. And—this is key, too—the author must submit to the freedom of the reader. To write and be read, she must give up the desire to predetermine the reader's comprehension in any absolute way and make herself vulnerable to the reader's interpretation. This is an important point, for, in all religions that consign God's words to a holy book, that very consignment presupposes, even establishes, a willingness on the part of the Creator to submit his or her expressions to the interpretive action of his or her readers. The author can try to seduce, but cannot force, the reader's understanding. For the reader can always shut the book. The irony in Socrates's case is that we only remember him because of Plato's writing. Whatever Socrates might have thought of the inefficiencies and possible abuses of printed words, it is through his disciple Plato's printed words that we know anything at all about Socrates's objections. Likewise, Muslims know about Allah, Buddhists know about Shakyamuni Buddha, Jews about Yahweh, and Christians about Jesus largely because the Divine was written about in a human book and because readers then responded by projectively animating God from the page.

Socrates's irony points to what I have been calling the productive paradox of reading, for, while reading can be a technology of alienation or distance that places the printed page between a person and the actual world and can make people want to shout "Put down that book and talk to me!," reading also bridges the gap of that alienation. "I'll just spend the day in bed with the Word," said my six-year-old brother. Any reader will tell you that some of her best friends have been found in books. For many booklovers, the projective communion of reading is solace in an otherwise alienating world. If reading arose and became widespread through modernity and the printing press's mass production of affordable books, and if modernity involves the alienation of individuals from a sense of deep belonging in an organic community by means of the ever-increasing industrialization, technologization, and commercialization of private life, then reading has both contributed to that alienation *and* served to mollify it.

BECAUSE SOCRATES FOCUSSED on the losses of the writer as compared to the teacher in face-to-face dialogue, he didn't pay much attention to the gains of the reader. Writing can indeed alienate words from the mouth that spoke them, and it does emphasize the gap between the origin and destination of an utterance, but reading these words can also create new belonging. Because texts involve both of these possibilities, both the alienation and the new belonging, they can produce individual and social change. Let me give an example. My parents were members of a missionary organization that

began its work in south-central Ethiopia in the 1920s. The
first missionaries worked in an area known as Walaitta, where
only the local government officials and Orthodox priests
could read Ethiopia's official language, Amharic. The regent,
later Emperor Haile Selassie, sent these first missionaries to
this region populated by animists largely to avoid competi-
tion between the Protestant missionaries and the Ethiopian
Orthodox Church, which was centuries old in northern parts
of the country but only superficially and recently imposed
upon the Walaitta people. The Walaitta language had not yet
been transliterated, and very few of the local people could
speak, let alone read, Amharic. This was the language of
Selassie's tribe that had colonized them in the nineteenth
century and the language closest to Walaittinia into which
the Bible had been translated. In an effort to assimilate the
Walaitta people into the Amhara-Orthodox hegemony, the
Amhara provincial governors outlawed teaching or publishing
in the local vernacular and discouraged missionaries from
learning it. Not for another fifty years would there be significant parts of the Scriptures available in Walaittinia.

So, imagine the challenges these circumstances posed for
the missionary enterprise of spreading the Protestant gospel,
with its central dictum of reading the Bible for oneself; how
many obstacles there would have been for Walaitta people to
hear the basic ideas of this new form of Christianity, let alone
decide to become believers. Interested Walaitta people would
have had to pick up whatever ideas of the Protestant faith they
could gather either through translators, through whatever
halting Walaittinia the foreigners had picked up, or through
whatever faulty Amharic they themselves had learned. If they
wished to read the Bible for themselves, then, they would essen-

tially have to betray their families, friends, and neighbours by learning the oppressor's Amharic language. They would do this, not to align themselves with their overlords, but so they could learn the language well enough to get a comprehensive grasp of the religion the foreigners were speaking about. So, identifying with the missionaries' gospel message meant alienating yourself from your own people, as well as risking the ire of the ruling Amharas by identifying with the foreigners' rival form of Christianity. It's amazing that anyone was willing to undertake this complex and dangerous process. But they did, and in the thousands. What's remarkable in the existing accounts we have of people's negotiation of this process is the key role played by literacy and books.

There was a diviner named Ato Chelleke, for example, who died years before the arrival of missionaries in his area (Cotterell 115). This famous seer had uttered a wild vision to his startled listeners in a part of Gofa province where no version of Christianity—whether Orthodox or Protestant—was yet known. In this vision, he predicted that men carrying hooked sticks would arrive by way of the river and that they would approach him in the shade of his sacred *wanza* tree. They would bring with them a book with golden pages from which they would speak in loving detail, and they would then build big houses in each village so that all who entered these houses would save their souls. Sure enough, months after Ato Chelleke's prediction, some early Walaitta Christians followed the river valley into Gofa province, and they carried walking sticks with a shepherd's crook at the top. Illiterate themselves, they brought with them a teaching aid they had received from the missionaries back in Walaitta called a "wordless book." They talked with Ato Chelleke about a new way of life, and to help him understand it, they pointed to a black page for sin, a red page for blood sacrifice, a white page for a cleansed heart, and a gold page for the heaven that awaited the repentant sinner. When the old prophet saw the final gold page, he knew it would not be long until the community would gather together to build a big house in his village.

So a wordless book played a key role in the Gofa people's predisposition toward Christianity—it opened them, made them vulnerable to the Walaitta evangelists' words. What interests me in this story is that, like the boy in the bunk bed, the people are not yet readers when the book arrives. In fact, books are unknown among them. They may have heard of books from neighbouring peoples or from the colonizing Amharas, but they have no books of their own. Nonetheless, there is a posture of openness, of receptivity, of respect for a kind of authority represented in the wordless book. Ato Chelleke's prophecy prepared the Gofa people for the arrival of the golden book that signalled massive social and cultural change. It signalled the building of a whole network of big houses or church communities in villages throughout Gofa province: today there are hundreds of thousands of Protestant Christians in Gofa, all foretold on Ato Chelleke's golden page.

Let me give another Ethiopian example of the link between literacy and cultural politics. In his autobiography, Ato Markina Meja, one of the earliest Protestant converts in the Walaitta area, records that he was required by the elders of the newly formed Walaitta church to demonstrate his readiness for baptism by reading aloud several Biblical passages. This was the sign of preparedness: the ability to read the Bible in Amharic, the oppressor's language. Think of it, a young Walaitta man in the 1930s, declares his intent to depart from

his people's long-standing animist beliefs and to join himself
to a new understanding of everything—God, humanity,
the world, his own community—by showing that he can
read Amharic words from a page and know what they mean.
The capacity to distinguish himself as an individual and
separate himself from his pagan neighbours comes through
reading. Reading marks the cut from the old and the identification with the new. His encounter with the modern and
alienating technology of reading marks a distance between
him and the organic, oral community of his childhood.

But this cut does not leave him permanently isolated. It puts
him in touch with what reading theorist Stanley Fish would
call a new interpretive community. It addresses and compen-
sates for his alienation not just by introducing him to other
readers in the new Walaitta church, but also by introducing
him to the community of voices that compose the Bible. He
meets Jesus Christ, St. Paul, and King David. He makes the
acquaintance of Thomas the skeptic, Joseph and Daniel the
interpreters of dreams, and Ezekiel the book-eater—about
whom I will have more to say in chapter five. He meets what
the writer of the epistle to the Hebrews calls a "great cloud
of witnesses"—a virtual, more abstract form of community,
granted, but nonetheless one that is every bit as real.

My point here is that reading does a painful and a positive
thing at once. It creates the isolated individual who extracts
herself from the group, but that isolation is not as alienated as it looks, for reading is also a connection to others, an
imaginative connection to the writer and to other readers by
means of the tracks the writer has left on the page. And in
this double process there lies the potential for the reader to
be changed by what he or she reads. This change is not simply

a mental shift, for it involves identification with a different community or communities, as the stories of Ato Markina Meja and the eight-year-old Dionne Brand show. It necessitates a reader who is willing to risk vulnerability and openness to the unfamiliar and unknown, and it involves a lifting of the reader out of the horizons of his or her immediate existence and an introduction to a wider or different set of possibilities. We can enter into Socrates's dialogue with Phaedrus about the dangers of literacy because Plato wrote it down in a book. The six-year-old boy in the bunk bed knew he could escape the scary rowdiness of the dormitory by placing the King James Bible on his lap and, through it, connect to the set of figures who sustained his family early every morning. The little girl seeking sweets was introduced to Touissaint L'Ouverture and the cultural politics of the African diaspora.

NOW, IN THE CASES OF ATO CHELLEKE and my six-year-old brother, I've highlighted the posture of the pre-literate reader in front of the sacred book. I think that it can be difficult for people in our culture, who have access to more cheap books than we know what to do with, to recall a sense of deep respect or reverence for books and especially the sacredness of scriptures. The Bible itself has become remarkably commodified over the past twenty or so years. It used to be that you might choose between two or three English translations of the Bible, but of late we have seen the niche marketing of Bibles for each and every taste: there are not just red-letter edition Bibles, illustrated Bibles, condensed Bibles, or amplified Bibles, but there are now a whole raft of specialized study Bibles: prophecy study Bibles, teenagers' study Bibles, study Bibles for the working person and for the spirit-filled woman—not to mention the host of Bible versions available on the web. Bible peddlers, like the manufacturers of bottled water, have realized that you can create whole new markets by packaging the product in an array of new containers. As a result of this overwhelming commodification, we have a hard time retaining any of the sense of awe and expectation Ato Chelleke, Ato Markina Meja, or my six-year-old brother felt before the open book. To a large extent, we have become cynical about books and reading. We reduce our reading of books to the information we can derive from them, to facts and arguments that support our own pre-existing views, or we approach them critically, confident of our modern sophistication in comparison to the outdated or polit-ically incorrect views of writers now dead or superannuated.

I'm not saying that we shouldn't derive information from reading or that we should not maintain a sharp, critical engage-ment with the texts we read, but I do think that if we are to rediscover a spiritually nourishing experience of reading, we need to rediscover the posture of the Gofa diviner and the little boy before the open book: a posture of openness and expectation, of anticipating something new from the book, an intention to reach through the technology of print on the page to connect with something larger than and outside of our own sphere of experience—toward God, toward a community of other readers, toward a set of understandings that could very well change us and everything we know. Augustine, who had been surprised and frustrated by St. Ambrose's silent reading, went on to become an impassioned silent reader and one of the first people to formulate a careful and system-atic approach to reading. In his book, *On Christian Doctrine*, he declares that charity is both the method and the object of reading Scripture. Whoever, therefore, claims to understand the text and doesn't build up love for God and neighbour, doesn't get it at all. But whoever learns charity from her reading, even if she mistakes what the author of a specific passage intended, has not been deceived (Augustine 30). To paraphrase Augustine, we might say that we read in order to develop right posture—the openness, vulnerability, and expectation toward the Other that is fundamental to charity—and we adopt a charitable posture in order to understand the book.

In this sense, then, the posture I'm sketching here necessitates, ultimately, the possibility of not just reading but of *being read by* the book. A spirituality of reading that has any hope of addressing Bob the red-bearded Buddhist postman's objections demands a posture of humility and vulnerability before the open book. You can't have an open book and a closed reader, for a closed reader closes the book, even if the page is ostensibly open. An open reader is driven by a kind of recognized need, a deep longing that is willing to undergo the alienating mediation of print and to reach imaginatively through the words on the page toward the real presences beyond them. There are reading postures that are antithetical to spiritual life: the reader who hallucinates the world of a book as if it were her own already-established reality, or the reader who gathers facts and arguments from books to show his superiority to others or who, in turn, assumes that his vicarious knowledge from one book makes him wiser than the next book he reads. If reading is to have any impact, it requires a posture of expectation and receptivity.

This posture is not naïve. It does not sit wide-eyed before any and every book, assuming all are equally good and true. A spiritually healthy posture combines suspicion with its hermeneutics of affirmation. I would, however, call this

posture discerning rather than critical. Every word has
several definitions, but the first definition for "critic" in my
Canadian Oxford Dictionary is "a person who censures," the first
under "critical" is "making or involving adverse or censor-
ious comments or judgments," and the first under "criticism"
is "finding fault; censure." These fault-finding definitions
appear before we get to more constructive definitions for
criticism, such as analyzing, reviewing, or making an assessment. By comparison, discernment comes from the Latin,
dis-cernere, which means to divide or sort out. *Cenere* means to
sift through and select. A common synonym is "to diagnose."
Paul Smith, in *Discerning the Subject,* notes that "cern" has two
rarely used English verb forms "to cern" and "to cerne," the
first meaning "to accept an inheritance or patrimony" and
the second "to encircle" or "to enclose." So he sees discernment as the process of liberating or sorting out what has been
enclosed, what has been encircled by inheritance or patrimony.

This set of definitions highlights precisely what reading can
do: reading can be a process of discernment, where the reader
discerns the book and the book discerns the reader. By placing a
mediating technology between the reader and his or her given
world, reading sorts the reader out from his patrimony, perhaps
even diagnoses her inheritance. The reader needs to be open
for this process to happen. But the next important step is that,
having been discerned, the reader needs to become discerning.
The reader needs to develop the capacity to sort out influences,
sources of wisdom, and constructive knowledge from texts
and influences that can cause harm. Although both "criticism"
and "discernment" account for similar processes of sorting,
evaluation, and decision, criticism emphasizes two things
not emphasized by discernment: fault-finding and judge-

ment. The qualification to be a critic seems to be the capacity to find fault, whereas discernment emphasizes liberation, the release of what was enclosed and tied to a heavy inheritance.

The difference in posture between the critical and the discerning reader is profound. The critic establishes his credentials by seeing a failure, which involves two dangers—that his own identity as a critic depends on the pursuit of others' errors and on not seeing or admitting his own. This is a cynical position to be in. The critic must find others' errors, but she must not find her own failings, otherwise she undermines her own critical authority. The discerning reader, on the other hand, separates out what was formerly enclosed and suppressed. In this sense she enacts a hermeneutics of suspicion, looking for the meanings hidden beyond or beneath the conscious surface. She diagnoses because she recognizes symptoms of failure and suppression that are part of our human patrimony. Discernment is self-reflexive. But it also performs a hermeneutics of affirmation because it seeks the enclosed and suppressed in order to liberate them. I emphasize the importance of discernment because it shows us how it is possible to maintain a posture of expectation and receptivity that is neither overly judgemental nor completely naïve.

A six-year-old boy in bed with the Word, a young Walaitta man who must read Biblical passages in his oppressor's language, an eight-year-old girl leaning over a drawer of sweets and falling into the face of a book: in all cases, the open book generates movement within the reader. In the first instance, the technology of print produces a division or dis-cernment of the reader from the organic community of face-to-face speech—the little boy from his family, me from my ancestors, and Ato Markina Meja from his friends and neighbours. But in the second instance, the very losses of this alienation are compensated for by the establishment of a new kind of belonging: for the boy, if not with his family, then with the realization that he has ways to commune with them across time and distance; for the eight-year-old girl with the history of slavery and her African genealogy; for the Walaitta man, a new belonging among the nascent group of Protestant believers. Reading is spiritual because it simultaneously emphasizes and spans this divide between the self and other, between the reader and the author, between the reader and the world, between the reader and God. We develop right posture when as readers we recognize the structure of absence or distance across which we long to pass, when we recognize our limitation and isolation, and when we discern the suppressed or hidden possibility of connection and belonging to the Other who seemed so far removed.

FOUR

The Structure

KAREN ARMSTRONG'S LIFE kicked to smithereens her capacity to believe in God and religion. So it seems ironic that she has become famous as a religion writer and, if not ironic, then remarkable that her biographies of St. Paul, Muhammad, and Buddha, in addition to her histories of God, Islam, and fundamentalism, are not revenge for her experience of the failures and abuses of religion. It is striking that, having experienced nothing but the

# of Absence

absence of God, her books trace people's experiences of God's presence everywhere.

She certainly started out with a sincere desire for a vibrant religious experience. Her memoir, *The Spiral Staircase: My Climb out of Darkness,* describes how she determined, at the age of seventeen and against her parents' better judgement, to become a Roman Catholic nun. Rather than being led, however, through her vows of obedience, contemplation of the

Scriptures, and ascetic disciplines to an experience in which the distractions of the world were stripped away and she entered into a deep intimacy with God, she found herself over the next seven years increasingly alienated from others, from herself, and whatever God might be. Her superiors were rigid and loveless, and submission to their authority became increasingly absurd. Once, when she and the other young postulants were being trained in their sewing skills, she damaged the convent's new sewing machine, and she was sent by a furious Mother Albert into the next room to practice on an older machine for half an hour every day. But, Karen pointed out, the machine had no needle. "How dare you!" replied her mistress. "Don't you know that a nun must never correct her superior in such a pert manner...You will go to that machine next door, Sister, and work on it every day, needle or no needle, until I give you permission to stop" (Armstrong 34–5). And here is the truly damaging part: Karen did go to that room and treadle away on the empty machine for the next two weeks, telling herself all the while that, however pointless the exercise might look to the human eye, this was the way of obedience and it would lead her somehow to God. She was taught to doubt her own mind.

Other circumstances reinforced her self-distrust. She began to have fainting spells, moments when the world would grow bleary, a strange smell of sulphur would permeate her nostrils, and waves of colour would distort everything she could see. Rather than inquiring into her health when she keeled over during Mass or in the refectory, her superiors accused her of histrionics, of emotional indulgence and exhibitionism. Nuns were not to be wilting Victorian ladies, they insisted, but tough soldiers of Christ, whose virile spirits exercised strict control over their emotions and bodily functions. Karen promised to try harder and to pull herself together. But the spells only increased, along with her superiors' irritation. Finally, the day came when she realized that she was a failure. She had done her best to give her life to God, but God didn't seem to want it, and neither did her religious order. She did not have what it took to be a nun.

So she left the convent and enrolled at Oxford, doing the only other thing she knew how to do outside of the convent: study literature. Armstrong says that she was a competent student, but, having learned to distrust her own mind, she had nothing original to say, with the result that she wrote essays that merely sorted through the ideas of others. Her self-doubt had dried up her creativity, deprived her of confidence that she had resources within herself worth tapping. It made her unwilling to pursue the questions that really interested her. In addition to being trained in the convent to doubt her own mind and heart, the fainting spells intensified during her years at Oxford. Misguided by psychiatrists, she spent years in psychotherapy, taking drugs for stress and anxiety. Once she was institutionalized after trying to commit suicide with the sleeping pills she had been given for insomnia; several times she woke up in hospitals after having fainted in public places. Her internal world in disarray, her external world kept falling apart. Her competent essays carried her all the way through the requirements of an undergraduate and graduate degree at Oxford, but she did not pass the final examination of her doctorate. Eventually, then, she failed in academe as well as in religion. She tried a third career as a teacher in a secondary school. Again she was competent, but her uncertain health made her miss so many days of teaching that she was eventually let go. She seemed to be unemployable.

To add insult to injury, she learned during her years as a teacher that her spells of fainting and amnesia were the results of epilepsy, not some psychosis, and the drugs she had been taking had only muddied the waters. This shocking discovery was the beginning of her recovery, however, for it relieved her of blaming herself for her failures. Healing and mental stability were no longer a matter of "getting hold of herself." It was an indescribable relief to know that the sulphuric odours, the strange visions, and strangely coloured auras she had experienced in her fainting spells were acknowledged by others, common symptoms of a known disease.

In the end it was reading that led her into a fulfilling life— into a creative vocation, a new self-knowledge, and a productive spirituality. As part of the process of sifting through and coming to terms with her painful life, Armstrong wrote a book, *Through the Narrow Gate,* about her convent years and her eventual loss of faith. She was surprised when the book did not merely creep onto the dusty shelves of the religion section at the back of bookstores: it became a popular sensation in Britain. Something about her story as an ex-nun caught the public imagination, and it soon got her invitations from television studios to speak about the ways religion abused women, how its patriarchal and puritanical impulses repressed femininity, freedom, sexuality, independent thinking, and individuality. Although she was nervous about appearing before the camera, she was glad to accept these invitations. She needed work, and here was a way of being compensated, in hard cash, for the suffering she had undergone and, at the same time, to get a little of her own back on the institutions that had caused her so much harm. Soon she was being asked to write television series, and then books, about the patriarchs of heavy religion, notoriously anti-woman figures such as St. Paul and Muhammad.

But something happened to Armstrong in the process of study, in her reading of these figures, that disallowed the fiery rebuttals or witty dismissals television viewers expected from an atheist ex-nun talking about St. Paul's or Muhammad's treatment of women. Whereas she started these projects as polemics that would set the record straight about these misogynists, something unexpected happened as she engaged in the research and writing. To her surprise, she found herself drawn to these unsalutary men; the process of research filled them out from cardboard stereotypes and made them into three-dimensional characters. She writes of her research on *Muhammad*: "I had to make a daily, hourly effort to enter into the ghastly conditions of seventh-century Arabia, and that meant that I had to leave my twentieth-century assumptions and predilections behind...It required a constant concentration of mind and heart that was in fact a type of meditation" (278). She says that this kind of meditation involves what theologians of many faith traditions have called *kenosis* or self-emptying and that it leads to *ekstasis* (Greek for "standing outside"). She insists that these impressive-looking terms don't signal some kind of exotic transcendence, but simply that we are momentarily liberated from the confines of our own egos, the small range of our own experiences. It was reading that alerted her to this process. "I have noticed," she writes, "that when I am full of resentment, anger, or egotistic distress, I cannot work properly. The texts do not open themselves to me" (299–300). She should know, she who has so many good reasons for resentment and anger.

By contrast with her days of failed reading at Oxford, her subsequent study of religious traditions, undertaken outside of the authoritative structures of the church and the university, has shown her that "a disciplined attempt to go beyond the ego brings about a state of ecstasy. Indeed, it *is* in itself *ekstasis*. Theologians of all the great faiths have devised all kinds of myths to show that this type of *kenosis*. . .is found in the life of God itself. They do not do this because it sounds edifying, but because this is the way that human nature seems to work. We are most creative and sense other possibilities that transcend our ordinary experience when we leave ourselves behind" (279). She was brought to this new creativity and energy by a new reading practice, by the posture of attention and openness to the Other that was possible only when she had disentangled her self-confidence and self-respect from the institutions that had undermined them.

What intrigues me about Armstrong's story is that this opening up of the self, this vulnerability to otherness, does not come about by means of something overtly religious or pious. It is simply the product of committing herself to reaching toward an understanding of the mind of another person without commandeering them into her own framework. It is the product of paying fierce and generous attention to others *as others*, allowing them to be other than who we expected them to be. And, more than this, that generous attention can be extended across enormous gaps in time, space, and culture in a way that is powerfully relevant today. Armstrong did the work of reading about and trying to understand Muhammad during the *fatwa* against Salman Rushdie and the build-up to the Gulf War of 1991, and, since publishing her book on the Prophet, she has become a regular speaker on Islam, trying to help post-9/11 people regain an understanding of its founder that has not been distorted by either

extreme Islamicism or Western Islamophobia. Her experience of ecstasy occurred in relation to another real person far
removed in time and culture, and it did not lead her to transcend or abandon the social and political world. Rather, it led
her more deeply *into* the world; it made her more rather than
less relevant to the world. Reading, the experience of being led
out of herself, paradoxically confirmed her in herself in a way
that had always been previously blocked. This whole paradigm
of *kenosis* and of *ekstasis* that can occur in the act of reading,
then, highlights a paradox in relations between self and Other
because it emphasizes what I call the structure of absence.

⸫ IN THE CLOSING PAGES OF HER BOOK, Armstrong
tries to explain how she can experience such powerful admiration and affinity for religious figures such as Muhammad or St.
Paul and yet not believe in God. How can she espouse spiritual
concepts such as *kenosis* and *ekstasis* without being a religious
person, without having much trust in mystical theories of
transcendence, or a basic faith in God? She turns to the structure of absence to explain: "the very absence I felt so acutely
was paradoxically a presence in my life. When you miss somebody very intensely, they are, in a sense, with you all the time.
They often fill your mind and heart more than they do when
they are physically present" (301). Regardless of all the certi-
tudes that religious doctrines put forward, regardless of all the
laws and principles, even the most confident religions claim
that very few people have seen God directly. Since most of us
have never seen God and are unlikely to, we live in the structure
of absence, gathering what information we can from others
and the world around us. Reading gives us concrete experience of this structure of absence and how it can be filled with

presence. Reading simultaneously emphasizes and bridges the structure of absence. It reminds us that we are cut off from the voice we are listening to, that we are alone. It also reminds us of the solitude of the Other, of other people, of the author, and it makes us reach responsively toward that absent Other. I propose that this experience of presence-in-absence that is fundamental to reading is precisely parallel to the experience of prayer. Perhaps this is why reading—think of the prayer books common to many religious traditions—has such a long history of being associated with prayer. There is something crucial to the experience of absence, to the recognition that the Other is not within my grasp or comprehension, that keeps me humbly aware of my own limited reach and of my longing for contact with, perhaps even a response from, the Other.

Socrates worried that when words are put into books they will go out into the world like orphans without the protection of their parents, and his worry indicates his concern with the structure of absence between the word and its author, between the meanings readers take from a book and whatever meanings its author intended. But it seems to have been Augustine who was the first to notice that this structure of absence is endemic to language itself. Augustine recognized that words are not identical with the things to which they refer; rather, they stand in place of those things. In fact, they are signs that we use to refer to things in their absence. He develops this very postmodern-sounding idea in *On Christian Doctrine,* one of the first systematic theories of reading in Western culture. Based on this distinction between the sign and its referent, Augustine goes on to distinguish between *use* and *pleasure.* If the point of living in the world is eventually to come to our true home in God, he reasons, then the things of this world need to be read as signs pointing toward that final destination. We should not get confused and become so engrossed in the things in this world that we lose sight of our ultimate end. We should use the things of this world, he says, to take pleasure in its Creator. And this means, in the context of reading, that people should use the Scriptures, as well as other books, to take pleasure in God. We must not cross up our priorities, Augustine says, and become worshippers of the book, which is only a sign that points toward God. That would be to fall in love with the Valentine card instead of the person who sent it. The purpose of reading and of life in general, for Augustine, is to learn to love God and the people around us. When we are motivated by love's longing, we need not be afraid of passages in Scripture that are difficult to understand, because readers who are compelled by a burning love for God and others will do the hard work of interpreting a challenging passage carefully, while lazy readers will just skip over the passage or close the book.

And then Augustine makes a statement that—for all the wrong reasons—leaps off the page for me: "books when they are understood, hold their readers to them *in a certain way*, and when they are not understood, are not troublesome to those not wishing to read" (Augustine 133, my italics). Basically, Augustine is saying here that people who don't understand difficult passages are likely to close the book, and that's fine because then they can't do too much damage to our understanding of God's words. But for people whose passion for God makes them willing to work hard in understanding a difficult passage, the book will take on a kind of magnetism that will hold them to it *in a certain way*.

Augustine here sounds something like the French philosopher Simone Weil who argued, in terms that anticipate

Karen Armstrong, that there is a link between serious study and the life of prayer. For if prayer is the ability to pay attention to God and to others around us and to the goings-on of the world in which we live, and if prayer involves the capacity to maintain that attention over an extended period, then the concentration and attentiveness that are required to work on math problems or to study geography are good practice for prayer (Weil 66, 70). Augustine hints at the same idea here: our minds go all over the place, hither and yon. Reading can provide a focus for the mind. Impassioned reading, reading fuelled by a powerful yearning for God, can help us learn concentration, teach us to pay attention.

But I said that Augustine's statement leaps off the page for me, and I have to admit that it does so for rather shabby reasons. When I first read Augustine's remark about books holding readers to them in a certain way, I heard a loud echo in his words that came from somewhere else—not from Augustine, not from the context of his life in what's now northern Egypt, not even from the context of his discussion of how we should approach the reading of the Scriptures. Of course, as for most readers, the echo came from my own context. I was sitting at my desk, my eyebrows knotted in concentration, my elbows on the desktop and my face resting in my hands, when my eyes came across this passage from Augustine. And it was as if Jacques Derrida banged upon the door to my study and shouted, "Just like I said—*in a certain way!*" You see, I was just then teaching a class in modern critical theory, and we were reading Derrida's first widely known essay of 1966, "Structure, Sign and Play in the Discourse of the Human Sciences." In 1966 Derrida, the young, white-haired French philosopher, jarred the world of humanistic studies during a conference at Johns Hopkins University when he insisted that Western culture is founded upon a metaphysics of absence, not one of presence. After shocking his listeners with his dismantling of what many at the time understood to be the bedrock of Western culture, Derrida pronounced the words that I heard echoing in the phrase I read from Augustine. "What I want to emphasize," said Derrida, "is simply that the passage beyond philosophy does not consist in turning the page of philosophy but in continuing to read philosophers *in a certain way*" (Derrida 967, emphasis in original).

Now, the echo I'm reporting here is audacious and gross misreading. I don't understand Latin well enough to know exactly what meanings shifted when Augustine's words were translated into English with the phrase "in a certain way"; nor do I read French well enough to evaluate the nuances that are missed when Derrida's statement is translated into the phrase "in a certain way." So here's what's happening: I'm an English reader, reading in the very uncertain territory of translated words, and I'm hearing an echo between the two statements. They bump into each other in a way that I want to explore. What did Augustine mean by "in a certain way" and what did Derrida mean by the same phrase, I wonder to myself, even though I know they didn't use exactly the same phrase, that they wrote what they wrote in different languages and radically different cultural contexts. I'm doing exactly what Socrates dreaded and what readers often do: making connections that the authors couldn't possibly have intended. And I can do this because they're both—Augustine and Derrida—absent, literally dead. I can't consult them directly, and I therefore pursue this echo through several intermediate layers and without appealing to their intentions.

When Derrida says we shouldn't turn the page of philosophy entirely but that we should read it *in a certain way*, I understand him to mean that we shouldn't throw the baby out with the bathwater. In this early speech and in much of Derrida's subsequent writing, he has intensely examined the ramifications of the observation Augustine had made fifteen centuries earlier, which is that words are not linked in any absolute way to their meanings. They are signs that stand, precisely, for something else. Signs work by convention, Augustine had noted; they are commonly agreed upon among people. Instead of taking several hours to draw ten thousand pictographs of warriors on piles of clay tablets to show how many enemy soldiers were approaching the city, the earliest writing we know about allowed Mesopotamian army commanders to make two or three quick marks on a page in a matter of seconds and send runners to organize their battalions for defence. And here is Augustine's and Derrida's point: the quick marks on the page stand in for the absence, luckily, of the ten thousand attackers. The purpose of making signs about them is precisely that they're not here yet, but we need to know about them coming. Herein lies Derrida's injunction to read philosophy in a certain way: writing, language, operates not upon a fullness of presence but upon a dynamics or metaphysics of absence. Derrida went on, throughout the rest of his career, to show how far-reaching this insight is. Because words are not linked inherently or absolutely to their meanings, but only by convention, we begin to see how they become meaningful only by comparison and differentiation from each other. You can check this out for yourself: look up a word, any word, in the dictionary, and you will find that it is defined by comparison and difference from other words.

For example, the word "certain," since that's the key term in the two statements I'm meditating on, has several definitions in my big, blue-covered *Canadian Oxford Dictionary*. Definition 1a reads "confident, convinced (*certain that I put it there*)" and this is followed by 1b: "indisputable; known for sure (*it is certain that he is guilty*)." So we know what "certain" means by associating it with confidence and conviction and by differentiating it from something that can be disputed. But these meanings don't seem quite right for the statements translated from Augustine and Derrida, which seem less absolutely certain than the certainty we're getting in these definitions. So let's move on to definition 4: "(of a person, place, etc.) that might be specified, but is not (*a certain lady; of a certain age*)." This fourth definition seems to capture the reduced or vague idea that's conveyed in the two statements: "certain," meaning not as confident or indisputable as we might wish, but nonetheless a nod toward certainty. There's a gesture to specificity and clarity that's not yet realized here, a reaching toward rather than an accomplishment of certitude. Definition 4 operates by association with definitions 1a and 1b (that is, it gestures toward the confidence and conviction they identify), but it also operates by differentiation from them: "certain" here is delayed in comparison to them, it sets them up as the goal that it has not yet reached. Books hold us to them in a certain way, or we ought to continue to read philosophy in a certain way—in both cases Augustine and Derrida seem to reach toward naming something specific, but they can't quite yet give it a name.

In fact, for Derrida, the "certain" way to read philosophy, and anything else, for that matter, is to remain alert at all times to the way in which meaningful utterance depends, not upon some solid ground or final guarantee, but on this ongoing, infinitely inventive play between words and the surrounding meanings to which they are compared and from which they always differ. Language, then, operates by means of Socrates's nightmare—by a metaphysics of absence: signs always stand in for things and concepts that are precisely not present, since the signs stand in for them in their absence. Words go out into the world unprotected by parents who can enforce their intended meanings. Written and spoken words do not refer to things and concepts directly, but by means of difference and comparison to other words. Now many people have understood Derrida's theory to be profoundly anti-theological. "In the beginning was the Word, the *Logos*," wrote John the gospel writer. It is Allah "who has sent down to you the Book," asserts Muhammad. "In it are verses basic or fundamental (of established meaning)" (Muhammed, *Surah* 3:7). Derrida has cited this idea as the source of the illusion of logocentrism, the idea that God's word is a transcendental sign that guarantees the meaningfulness of all of our human expressions. But let me return to Augustine's use of "in a certain way" to try to explain why I think Derrida's metaphysics of absence is an important and friendly, rather than unfriendly, insight for understanding reading as a spiritual activity.

The bad thing about books, according to Socrates, is that the writer can't defend or explain his utterances at the moment of reading. The reader attaches interpretations in the writer's absence—just as I have done in the absences of Augustine and Derrida. So reading consists of a strange paradox in which readers imagine themselves to be entering the mental world of the author precisely in the author's absence. It is, simultaneously, a powerfully intimate experience and an alienated one. The writing is what we have *instead of* the author. So, to return to Augustine, the process of reading "holds" the reader "in a certain way" because it requires an activity on the reader's part—a highly imaginative, responsive-projecting activity in which, from the clues on the page, the reader constructs his or her own mental image of the world depicted in the text. Augustine's reference to a "certain way" is unique and hard to pin down because it operates in the structure of absence.

I'm going to talk further about the reader's active engagement of the text in the absence of the author in a moment, but let me make a quick observation here about the faith or trust this structure of absence requires on the part of the author. The writer, in publishing her words abroad, commits an act of remarkable trust. She must believe that readers will make the effort of interpretation, that they will learn the technology of decoding letters and signs. She extends her words to the public, trusting that people will take them in good faith. Even the satirist trusts that readers will be willing to decode her tongue-in-cheek statements in keeping with the hints she has placed in the text to indicate that they must be taken ironically. So writers cannot live in Socrates's fear that their communications will be misinterpreted in their absence, for if they did, writers would never put their words into type. Instead, the writer must toss words upon the public page like bread upon the waters in order to make communication with the absent reader. We are back to Davidson's principle of charity.

This, then, is the faith that the Creator has in humans. If, as St. John put it, God is the Word that marked the Beginning of existence, then this expressive God has entrusted him or herself to human interpretation. The Creator has trusted that humans will read the book—the Scriptures, the book of nature, the books of their own honest impulses, the books of each others' lives—and read God's messages, imagine the Creator's world, project themselves toward God's mind. And God has done this in the best of faith, so that we as humans would have the freest choice possible. This kind of God will not hang over our shoulders like an over-controlling teacher to make sure we read his or her words in a preordained way. Rather, the Creator has given us maximum freedom in coming to our own interpretations of the world of signs we inhabit. As one who communicates, God has filled our world with signs and has called upon us to allow those expressions to hold us to God in a certain way.

   To CHANGE IMAGES A BIT, God-as-communicator is like a specific kind of writer, like a composer of music, whose text is inaudible until someone actually picks up a violin or a guitar and brings the silent text to life. This is what I understand incarnational thinking to be about: we humans become God's hands and feet as we enact or embody the sets of signs we have received about how to love God and live in the world. Roland Barthes, the French semiotician, has used this musical analogy to describe the absolute importance of the reader to the life of a text. Until someone with a violin or piano makes sounds from a sheet of music, the musical text is dead, silent (Barthes 1009). The text is inert until someone makes it come alive by performing it. And this act of performance enlivens the text, even brings its author back to life, in a manner of speaking. Without an interpreter—what George Steiner has called an "executant" (Steiner 7–8)—the text has no real presence, no vitality, no existence. We have this situation literally in the lost languages of the Etruscans: archeologists have found clay tablets in northwestern Italy covered with their writing, but because no one knows how to decode these texts, the tablets and their writers are dead. They have no life. The text needs to be sung, performed, embodied by the reader or musician in order for it to come to life.

The Canadian poet Don McKay has a wonderful poem in which he meditates upon the phenomenon of singing and its capacity for reaching into or across the structure of absence:

WINGS OF SONG

"We talk because we are mortal."
                                        —Octavio Paz
And because we aren't gods,
or close to gods,
we sing. Your breath steps
boldly into lift to feel that other breath
breathing inside it: Summertime, Amazing Grace. And when it stops
you sense that something fold back
into air to leave you listening
lonely as a post. Shall we call this angel?
Shall we call it animal, or elf? Most of us
are happy with a brief
companionable ghost who joins us in the shower or
behind the wheel. Blue Moon, Hound Dog, Life
Is Like a Mountain Railroad. When your voice
decides to quit its day job, which is mostly
door to door, to take its little sack of sounds
and pour them into darkness, with its
unembodied barks and murmurs, its refusal
to name names, its disregard for sentences,
for getting there on time,

or getting there,
or getting. (McKay 47)

This poem expresses, in reference to singing, what I consider
to be the fundamental wonder and value of the act of reading.
McKay's poem takes the next step beyond Roland Barthes's
comparison of reading with the performance of music, and
I think this next step is an intensely spiritual phase because
it involves the process of imaginative identification with an
Other. McKay's poem describes those everyday moments of
ekstasis, of what he calls "lift" (that's why he calls the poem
"*Wings* of Song"), when you find yourself singing in the most
mundane of places—the shower, alone in the car, on a ladder
washing windows—and you "feel that other breath / breathing
inside" the song you are singing, when you "are happy with
a brief / companionable ghost" who joins you in the song.
Or to put it differently, he describes the voice you can hear
in your head and which gives you the pleasure of sounding
much better than you do on your own. It's like hearing the
rock band or the orchestra in your head as you hum a tune, and
you have the experience of hearing your own voice fulfilled,
made beautiful, through its imagined harmonization with the
symphony or karaoke in your mind. Listen to someone singing
with their headphones on some time—the way they can be
so happy even though they're way out of tune—and you'll
have a good image of how this fulfilling projection works.

Reading is like this. It feeds a wonderful, life-warming
fantasy of self-enhancement that transforms your daily, "day
job" life, "which is mostly / door to door." Just as the fanta-
sized karaoke that elevates you into a rock star or into one
of the three tenors makes you sing up, makes you "step /

boldly into lift to feel that other breath / breathing inside
it" so that you fly on the wings of Pavarotti or k.d. lang or
Nat King Cole, so also the words on the page of a good book
can lift you from the muddle with its "unembodied barks
and murmurs, its refusal / to name names, its disregard for
sentences" and can let you sail on the wings of a well-crafted
sentence, on a clear insight, on a well-organized thought,
on a riveting image. This is the case because writing is organized and edited. It's idealized in that it doesn't offer the
whole cacophony of mental life. Even the freest appearing,
stream-of-consciousness writing is ordered and organized
by being fitted into words and sentences and grammar.

So the imaginative projection of reading constructs a kind
of intimacy with an ideal partner or friend. And this friendship,
in the most stimulating and pleasurable reading experiences,
is rarefied to its most ideal circumstances: your book-friend
or partner, the voice you are listening to and thinking with, is
clever, well-spoken, intelligent, insightful, witty, humorous,
ethically high-minded. If this friend did not possess some of
those qualities, you would close the book. This is to say that
when you're reading, you get to come up with ideas, understand complexities, and enter into experiences that you
couldn't have encountered alone. Like the junior violinist, you
get to pretend that you came up with Tchaikovsky's composi-
tion on your own. In this way, the imaginative projection of
reading or of singing transforms you, quite literally. Although
it would be easy to dismiss this activity as mere escapism, as
simply taking a break from the daily grind of reality, I want to
argue that by learning to follow a melody you would never have
invented on your own, by comprehending a concept or imag-
ining a world you had never heard of before, you are changed.

You become capable of actions, skills, and insights that were previously impossible for you. You have been changed, modified, through contact with an Other, who is a kind of companionable ghost, the other breath within your breath.

But there's more. This experience of appropriating the music of an Other, of projecting your own evolving understanding into the words of the author, is not an act of theft that takes something away from the composer. For, as I mentioned earlier, the notes on the musical staff, the words on the printed page, are dead and lifeless until someone appropriates them. In fact, the structure of absence means that the author himself is dead and the composer herself is irrelevant, until someone brings their work to life. The writer, in fact, *depends* on being appropriated by the reader or musician. This is all central to what I understand the spiritual life to be. We have inherited the transcripts of people's previous experiences of God and of trying to make sense of life, not just in holy books but in many texts—musical, literary, artistic—and we then enact them, perform them, by reading and interpreting them, by projecting ourselves into them, identifying imaginatively with them—to return to Georges Poulet's phrase, giving ourselves "on loan to them" (Poulet 45)—by understanding the shapes of our own lives in relation to them. If they stay alive at all, this is how cultural traditions stay alive. They stay alive because they are not hermetically sealed, closed off against new engagements, appropriations, and interpretations. The life of the Scriptures, the life of tradition depends upon this lively readiness to be taken up, enacted, and performed. *Play* is the word we use to describe what a musician does with a musical score. We play the texts we read into life.

This playfulness—don't miss the echo here of Derrida's essay title, "Structure, Sign, and *Play* in the Discourse of the Human Sciences"—is fundamental to the process of finding a book meaningful. By taking up its words, playing them on the tongue, trying out the various possibilities of its sentences, the permutations of its meanings, we bring the book to life. This is the "lift" of song: that by animating its words and notes in melody, rhythm, and harmony, we lever it from the grave of gravity and fill it with the buoyancy of wind and movement. And this playfulness does not constitute one of the trite versions of postmodernism that suggests any interpretation is okay, anything goes, the words on the page can mean any old thing the reader wants them to mean. No. For the imaginative projection at the heart of reading and spirituality is a contact with and response to a real Other. There *are* marks on the page put there intentionally by someone, and they limit the range of possible tunes and meanings that can be derived from them. The spirituality of reading is not just egocentric play, the kind of tuneless humming or whistling a person will do to ward off silence. No, what makes reading so close to spiritual practices, such as prayer and meditation, is that it is imaginative, responsive *kenosis*. It is projection toward an active Other whose traces, in the form of musical notes or words on the page, call out to the singer or reader to respond, to identify, to play along. It is this "companionable ghost" who calls us out of ourselves to a kind of self-enhancing *ekstasis* that, as Karen Armstrong's story of reading demonstrates, enriches and textures who we are right here, right now, in the real world.

NOW, ONE OF THE THINGS that should be coming into focus is how the structure of absence has multiple layers or stages. It's not just a simple matter of reading the words of an author in his or her absence, but also the text that the author leaves behind is multiply mediated. I referred to one example of this mediation when I noted that, according to all the major religions, the Creator has entrusted most of what we know about God to books written by human beings. Another example of mediation was central to my discussion of Augustine's and Derrida's uses of the phrase "in a certain way" when I called attention to the fact that this phrase is a chance echo between the translations of Augustine from Latin and Derrida from French. The point is that, more often than not, texts are mediated through multiple levels of production before they come to us. Think of the Judaic and Christian scriptures: despite the belief of some Christians that the King James Bible is the only authoritative Bible, these scriptures weren't written in Elizabethan English, nor were they written in a single language but in various dialects of Hebrew, Aramaic, and Greek. Christians above all else have a translated faith. Different from the Koran, which is understood to be authentic only in Arabic, the Christian scriptures—and this is true of Jewish, Buddhist, Hindu, and other scriptures—have spread because they have been translated into a whole variety of languages. And in all cases, including the Koran, it is understood that God did not write the book directly. Instead, the Creator chose or inspired human beings to write down his or her words into languages, cultures, and systems of meaning that they inhabited and understood. All the major religions teach that God employed humans to embody his or her expressions into print. My point here is that when we read, we read through the mediating presence of what Wayne Booth once called an "implied author": one whose voice and characteristics we derive from the tone and attitudes we encounter in the text. This means that we derive much of our knowledge about spiritual life through the words of other human pilgrims on the spiritual path.

Having indulged in a gross misreading of Augustine and Derrida, I might as well continue in the same less-than-respectable vein when I admit that one of my favourite fellow pilgrims on the spiritual path is a complete fake. He is not a real person but a composite figure made up, anachronistically, between an ancient poet and a twenty-first-century translator. This wonderful fellow pilgrim is known to me as Hafiz, a fourteenth-century Sufi poet who has been transmuted into English by a New York Jewish-American named Daniel Ladinsky, and in a poem entitled "Between Your Eye and This Page," this fake, composite Ladinsky-Hafiz writes about the implied author who stands in the structure of absence between us and the printed text:

> Between
> Your eye and this page
> I am standing.
> Between
> Your ear and sound
> The Friend has pitched a golden tent
> Your spirit walks through a thousand times
> A day.
> ...
>
> If you are still having doubts
> About His nearness
> Once in a while debate with God.
> Between
> Your eye and this page Hafiz
> Is standing.

Bump

Into me

More. (Hafiz 318)

This is a typical Ladinsky-Hafiz poem: clever, humorous, joy-
ful, pleased-with-himself, inviting, and always the mixture
of audacious and gentle love. But I am aware as I chuckle over
these lines that *what* I'm reading is a highly mediated text:
Hafiz wrote in the fourteenth century, roughly the same time
as Chaucer, in the city of Shiraz, Persia, in an Islamic culture
that was miles ahead of Chaucer's Christian England in literacy,
culture, and knowledge of the wider world. Hafiz was a Sufi,
that pre-Muslim sect that is mystical and liberal at the same
time, a sect that is famous for its whirling dervishes who seek
contact with God by spinning around in circles until most people
would be so dizzy they would lose their lunches. From the little
I know about Sufism, this is a faith that emphasizes the importance of embodied spiritual experience: ascetic practices are
not denials of the body's importance but recognition that your
body is one of the primary ways you perceive anything. Limiting
your diet to bread and water or enjoying gourmet feasts, cases of
wine, and an abundant sex life—all these bodily experiences tell
us about the focus and discipline or exuberance and generosity
of God in the world. But the medieval Sufis of Persia are also
famous for the rich poetic tradition that produced figures like
Jelaluddin Rumi and Shams-ud-din Muhammad Hafiz.

Hafiz has been translated into English by many translators for over two hundred years. But among these, Daniel
Ladinsky's translations stand out because Ladinsky has rather
scandalously transported these poems from their medieval
Persian ethos into new-age-style, Judeo-Christian-inflected

New York diction. He has Hafiz say things the historical Hafiz could not possibly have said. So, for instance, in one poem Ladinsky has Hafiz exclaim that "something major-league Wonderful" is about to happen, as if Hafiz regularly attended games between the New York Yankees and the Toronto Blue Jays; or, in another poem, his Hafiz asserts that fortune-telling charlatans would be better off "flipping soy burgers"—as if hamburgers, let alone vegetarian ones, were fairground food in medieval Persia. The audacity of these anachronistic translations irritates strict scholars of Persian poetry, but for me this very audacity is necessary to the playfulness I enjoy in these poems. They seem to me to catch the spirit, rather than the letter, of Hafiz. Ladinsky defends his outlandish translations by recognizing that some readers might take offense at his having "taken the liberty to play a few of these lines through a late-night jazz sax instead of from a morning temple drum," but he insists nonetheless that the word translation comes from the Latin "to bring across," and his goal is to "*bring across,* right into your lap, the wondrous spirit of Hafiz that lifts the corners of the mouth." He sees this as a "no-holds-barred task" (Ladinsky 5). There is a vivacity, an energy, a joy that comes out of Ladinsky's lack of concern for authenticity.

And I am not alone in my appreciation, because Ladinsky's translations have been quickly, even enthusiastically, translated, in their turn, into German, Japanese, Chinese, Spanish, Czech, Slovenian, and even back into Persian. Think of it: there are Persian readers who read Hafiz by way of a twenty-first-century author's New York English that has been re-translated back into Persian. The ultramodern feel of Ladinsky's Hafiz is catching the ear of twenty-first-century Iranian readers who find this voice recognizable and familiar and appealing, even though they have the original texts Hafiz wrote in ancient Persian. This phenomenon should not surprise us too much: think of the way Chaucer is difficult for contemporary English speakers to read and how his texts are "translated" into modern English, or, for that matter, how new translations of the Bible (we often call them paraphrases) are published every five or ten years to bring a renewed freshness to texts that can feel dated and irrelevant. Between us and any page we read, there is a structure of absence, and the task of the reader when he or she picks up the text is to *translate it*, bring it across, bring it to life, embody it, in the contemporary world. Otherwise, the wisdom it holds, the tradition it represents, remains voiceless and dead.

So between my eye and Hafiz's page, "I" is standing—an implied author who is a complex composite of a radical, sensual, and mystical fourteenth-century Persian poet named Hafiz and an irreverent new-age-and-ashram-loving American translator named Ladinsky. There *is* a personality in which I take great delight in these poems—a personality that rises up from the printed page and that utters wisdom and humour into my ear. This is the "Hafiz" I return to page after page and poem after poem, as I read my way, in a certain way, through his book of poems. This is the "Hafiz" who, in his own absurdly modern theology insists that we human beings are "God in drag." "You are the Sun in drag," Ladinsky-Hafiz writes in another poem, "You are God hiding from yourself...You are a divine elephant with amnesia / Trying to live in an ant / Hole. / Sweetheart, O sweetheart / You are God in / Drag!" (252). Come out and play, cries Ladinsky-Hafiz. Let the text of this poem free you from your fear, your sense of yourself as trapped and isolated; here I am, a friend, an imaginary playmate who longs for you to see the godlike beauty that I see in you. The composite "Hafiz" between my eye and the page is, what he calls, "the Friend": "Between / Your ear and sound / The Friend has pitched a golden tent / Your spirit walks through a thousand times / A day."

This is, indeed, the power and peculiar effect of reading. In the exchange between eye and page, between ear and sound, an image of a Friend (a character, an author, a narrative voice who is the reader's host or guide) is generated between us and the golden tent of the text. The audacity of Ladinsky's inauthentic translation of Hafiz simply emphasizes, or makes more visible than usual, the regular process by which this imagined personality of any text (the companionable ghost with whom we walk) is generated in the reading process. Think of how often this figure of the guide or companion reappears in literary and spiritual texts: Dante is guided by Virgil on his tours of heaven and hell in *The Divine Comedy*, the angel guides St. John's visions of the apocalypse in Revelations, Pilgrim has Talkative, then Hopeful, as companions on his way to the heavenly city in Bunyan's *Pilgrim's Progress*. Whether it's by an actual character in the book, or whether it's by means of an author's tone, choice of narrative voice, arrangement of subject matter; whether it's by the decisions made by editors, translators, publishers, marketing specialists or what have you: the text we read is mediated. There is an "I," a Friend, a spirit between us and the text, and the nature of that "personality" is a composite created by all the participants in the production and reception of the text.

This mediating presence resonates, again, with incarnational spirituality. God's word, according to Christian teaching, is expressed in human form, in the human life of Jesus, whose humanity makes the immensity and incomprehensibility of God something people can begin to understand. The humanity of Christ mediates divinity so it can be recognized by human beings. Human beings, in turn, become guides and companions to each other, embodying the Divine for each other. "I am / A hole in a flute / That the Christ's breath moves through—/ Listen to this / Music," writes Ladinsky-Hafiz (203). Reading emphasizes this process of mediation; it emphasizes what I have been calling the structure of absence. By doing so, however, it shows that it is, paradoxically, not solitary, even though we can sit and read by ourselves, for it always involves the mental, emotional, spiritual projection of an "I" between our eye and the page.

⊙ ONE OF THE THINGS that Ladinsky-Hafiz capitalizes upon in this and in many of his poems is the intimacy of this process of projection—the fantasy that Hafiz and his reader are the only two in the world at the moment and their contact ("Bump / Into Me / More") is sensuous like sex, like an all-night conversation between two friends, like the intimate ministrations of a lover to a hurt or wounded loved one: "I will turn myself into a / Forest / Herb," he writes in another of his poems, "If / You will / Apply me to your / Wounds" (310). This experience of intimacy is central to what I understand to be the spirituality of reading, for it is spiritual in the sense of eliciting and also addressing the longing to be meaningfully connected that is central to human spiritual desire. There is an erotic element to this desire for connection that Ladinsky-Hafiz expresses, not so much in the sense of genital sex (although his poems certainly include this dimension, too), but in the sense of the deep human need to be understood, to be known, to be held intimately, to know that one matters to somebody else. This spiritual element of reading as expressed in Hafiz is a fantasy of perfect understanding, the feeling that the "I" projected between my eye and the text is someone I understand readily and who knows and anticipates my deepest needs. When such a fantasy of intimacy occurs, my reading self is "opened"—my hopes, desires, needs are exposed and addressed—because I am not afraid of being trampled upon or criticized in front of others for triviality, banality, or ordinariness. This is the vulnerable posture of which I wrote in the previous chapter, the openness and humility that reading encourages and makes possible.

"I'll just spend the day in bed with the Word," said my six-year-old brother, and my family has chuckled appreciatively at his sweetness ever since. There are many of us who would love to spend a day, maybe even a life, in bed with the Word. We needn't be six years old in a dormitory to feel the need for the remarkable mixture of solitude and good company, silence and conversation, privacy and connectedness that is the magic of reading. We are constantly aware of the structures of absence in our lives: we all experience the feeling that anything like a loving Creator is far removed from the world in which we live. We all mourn the fact that the people we love may be far away, or, even worse, living right in the same house, sleeping in the same bed, sharing the same toothpaste, but nonetheless remote in spirit or emotion. We all fall prey to the fear that we may not measure up this time—that we aren't holy enough to become a nun, that we aren't smart enough to pass the exam, that we're not truly lovable enough to deserve a Friend. We all have days when we'd rather put on our pyjamas and snuggle back into the blankets, pillows, and sheets. When we need to get in bed with the Word. And what's remarkable is that it works. That the Word can work like a forest herb on the wounds we have sustained, that it can introduce us to the Friend in the golden tent, that it can provide us with a companionable ghost, so that we feel another breath breathing inside our own breath, and we can be lifted on the wings of a well-composed song. Reading is spiritual because it emphasizes and energizes the structures of absence, which are our condition as mortal human beings.

FIVE

Eating

IN MEDIEVAL JEWISH SOCIETY, the Feast of Shavout, which celebrated Moses's receiving the Torah from the hands of God, involved an initiation ceremony for boys who were about to learn to read. The boy in question was wrapped in a prayer shawl and taken by his father to the teacher. The boy would sit on the teacher's lap where he would be shown a slate on which were chalked some of the Hebrew alphabet, a passage from the Scriptures, and the words "May the Torah be your occupation." The teacher would

the Book

read each word, and the child would repeat it.

Then, the slate would be covered with honey

and the child would lick it clean, thereby

ingesting the holy words (Manguel 71).

   The child licking the slate was being taught

the same posture my six-year-old brother

had learned from my parents' early morning

quiet times. He was learning that the Word

is a kind of food, a necessary sustenance, like

the coffee they sipped as they ingested its

phrases. We digest the Word so that it gets

chewed up and absorbed into the very fibre, bone, blood, and tendons of our being. What was one element, words on a page, becomes absorbed, reconstituted into muscle, brain cells, saliva, hair follicles. This is incarnational thinking: that the Word doesn't merely remain ideas on a page, not merely instructions in a training manual, not simply the historical record of things long past or of abstractions in the mind, but that it becomes fused into the viscera of our bodies. The book we eat becomes us: shapes what we see, how we hear, what we perceive through touch or taste or smell. The object of eating the book is pleasure, rumination, and sustenance. Like contemplation, it is not rushed through but savoured and digested—tasted all the way through.

⁘ THIS JEWISH CEREMONY echoes the weird scenes of book-eating that recur in the Jewish scriptures. Book-eating launches the careers of several Hebrew prophets, including Jeremiah and Ezekiel, as well as John of Patmos in the Christian book of Revelations. Each of these men has a vision in which he is given a scroll to eat and, having eaten the book, he then sets out to communicate God's message to humanity. Each of these scenes is fascinating in its own right, but in the interests of brevity, I'll focus on the story of Ezekiel, where book-eating gets the fullest treatment. Ezekiel's career opens with a wild, psychedelic vision in which he is called to become a messenger of God to the Israelite exiles in Babylon who have assimilated to their pagan surroundings and have forgotten their mono-theistic covenant with God. In this vision, he sees four strange creatures with four heads and four wings each, and with eyes all over their bodies. Above them thunders the voice of Yahweh:

"You, son of man, listen to the words I say; do not be a rebel
like that rebellious set [of Israelites to whom I am sending
you]. Open your mouth and eat what I am about to give
you." I looked. A hand was there, stretching out to me and
holding a scroll. He unrolled it in front of me; it was written
on back and front; on it was written "lamentations, wail-
ings, moanings." He said, "Son of man, eat what is given to
you, eat this scroll, then go and speak to the House of Israel."
I opened my mouth; he gave me the scroll to eat and said,
"Son of man, feed and be satisfied by the scroll I am giving
you." I ate it, and it tasted sweet as honey. (Ezekiel 2:8 -3:3)

A footnote in my Jerusalem Bible explains that Ezekiel has been
called the "father of Judaism," and I suspect he might be known
in this way because of this scene of eating the book. Somewhere
at the base, at the very origin of the Judaic faith, is the eating
of the book. It is a difficult book of lamentations, wailings, and
moanings. But when it is eaten, like the boy licking the words
of the Torah from his teacher's slate, it tastes sweet as honey.

What a strange set of images! The eating of the scroll,
written back and front with sorrows. The call to speak to a
tough audience who are not likely to listen. And the sugges-
tion that Ezekiel will be sustained by having eaten the book of
grief, that he will have something worth saying by having eaten
it, and that the experience will be sweet to the taste. The scene
has many echoes in Jewish and Christian rituals and iconog-
raphy. The Jewish celebration of Passover involves the tasting of
the bitter herbs dipped in the brine of tears and the devouring
of the sacrificial lamb. Both are incorporated into the Christian
eating of the bread of the Eucharist, which is a consuming

of the Body of Christ, who was called the Word of God. What Christians eat in communion is the body of sorrow, of lamentations, wailings, and moanings—for the suffering and breaking of Christ's body on the cross incorporates human suffering and brokenness and embodies human vulnerability to death, pain, fragmentation, and disintegration. Add to this the belief that, in eating Christ's body of pain, humans sustain themselves: by identifying with, even consuming, the broken body, the broken Word, flawed people are somehow sustained and healed.

But the eating of the book also suggests, more generally, the contemplation of, the incorporation of the Word into readers' bodies. We digest the Word so that it is absorbed into our bodies. What was one element, words on a scroll back and front, becomes absorbed, reconstituted into muscle, bone, fingernails, lungs, and arteries. The result of eating the sorrowful book is, strangely, sweetness and sustenance. This eating is not rushed through but savoured and swallowed, ruminated upon, tasted for its richness and nuance. As the Carthusian Guigo II suggested in his outline of *lectio divina*, or sacred reading, spiritually nourishing reading is slow. It proceeds gradually from *lectio* or basic reading, to *meditatio* or meditation, then to *oratio* or enunciated prayer, and finally to *contemplatio* or mystical communion with God (Pennington 76–80, Casey 57–59). Each of these steps overlaps with the others, returns to the same passage, spends time ruminating upon it. Spiritual reading chews on difficult, even painful passages; it doesn't push them to the side of the plate nor does it swallow them whole.

BUT WHY SHOULD Ezekiel's and Jeremiah's and St. John's books be ones of sorrow? Isn't there room in spiritual reading for joy? celebration? triumph? What's so spiritual

about the negative stuff? I remember asking this question
in my first literature classes when I went to university: why
do so many of the great classics have to be depressing? Are
there no happy masterpieces? The regicides, patricides, and
suicides pile up from *Oedipus Rex* to *Hamlet,* from *Anna Karenina*
to *The Satanic Verses.* The same question has occurred to me
as I have been reading many of the spiritual classics: why do
suffering, pain, and self-denial have to be so central to these
books? *The Cloud of Unknowing, The Dark Night of the Soul, The
Cost of Discipleship*—isn't there any joy in the spiritual life? The
book Ezekiel is required to eat is a book of lamentations, wailings, and moanings; Jeremiah's name has become synonymous
with despair; John of Patmos eats from the same unhappy
book. Theirs is not a book about the purpose-driven life or the
power of positive thinking, nor is it about the habits of highly
effective people or how I'm okay and you're okay. It is not a
book of instructions, happy endings, jokes, erotic stimula-
tion, beautiful poems, or suggestions for self-improvement.

It is a book of grief, and there are good reasons why this
is so. Hard-hearted, cynical audiences are usually smart. You
can't tell them anything they haven't thought about before.
Critique, clever interventions, intriguing arguments, and brilliant analyses are the bread and butter hard-hearted people
chew up and spit out without stopping to breathe. The chink
in the armour of cynics, however, is sorrow. There is a "still, sad
music of humanity" that the poet William Wordsworth knew
about, and it pulsates deep in the heart, under the layers of bril-
liance and polish that we humans present to one another in our
everyday, I-can-take-care-of-it-myself lives. This sad music is
the awareness we have of not living up to the polish we present
to one another; the sadness we feel about not being able to

match our behaviour to our own values; the sorrow of living
in Babylon, in a world whose advertising and cynicism have
gotten inside of us and alienated us from what truly nurtures
us. It's an awareness of the way our innocence, our dreams to fill
out our potential, our capacities for generosity and creativity
have been stunted by our personal histories—by family systems
that shrivelled our confidence to even try to realize our abilities,
by political and economic systems that compromise our hopes
for justice and equity, by our own failures of nerve to hold out
for better things when cheap imitations offer ready substitu-
tions, by the frailty of being human and losing our best years to
bad health, depression, and the loss of loved ones. The book of
sorrows, of lamentations, wailings, and moanings, is a book we
all know by heart when we're honest with ourselves. It is a book
that cuts through the brilliant defences of the intellect and
finds a home in what David Lyle Jeffery has called "the broken-
hearted reader" (Jeffery 353–73). And, because it cuts to the
chase, because it separates the joint from the marrow, the book
of grief, rather than tasting only sour and bitter, can actually
nourish us. Strangely, as in Ezekiel's case, it can taste sweet
as honey. For in speaking honestly to our hurt, to our human
pain, the book of grief can put a healing hand upon the parts
of us that need desperately to be acknowledged and touched.

So it is possible to see how the book of grief can helpfully
address the broken and painful aspects of our lives. But surely
it is only a self-wounding, masochistic spirituality that would
make sorrow the only item on the reader's menu, is it not? Of
course. There are some benefits that come from the book of
grief, but there are other kinds of readerly benefits, and some
of them are actually pleasurable. There is, in keeping with
Ezekiel's book of sorrows, a *pleasure of devastation* that I'll talk

about first before I proceed on to the *pleasures of confirmation* and *surprise* that I think are important to a spirituality of reading.

First, the pleasure of devastation. I don't think I'll ever forget reading Fyodor Dostoevsky's *Crime and Punishment* when I was twenty-three years old. The book is too multi-layered and complex to supply an adequate account of it here, and even a summary sketch would take the rest of the space of this chapter. So let me try to convey a sense of the book's tone: the novel keeps you burning through the pages in a kind of fevered nightmare as you are drawn into the brilliant, unbalanced mind of a young nineteenth-century Russian student who robs and murders a rich pawnbroker to save his sister from being married off for money. As if it were yesterday, I remember finishing this powerful, fascinating, frightening novel, looking up in a daze from the chair in which I had been reading, and deciding I needed air. I needed to get outside. So I got on my bicycle and pedalled down to the park, where I locked up to a rusted metal bike rack and began to stroll around the lake. It was summer. I had just emerged from Dostoevsky's St. Petersburg. I had not realized it was summer. I had not realized it would be hot. I had just come from smoke-filled Russian tea shops, where restless, radical students muttered under their breaths and tried to avoid the searching gazes of the Czar's police. I looked in amazement across the park lawn at two young guys, stripped to their waists in the hot sun, floating a Frisbee back and forth between them. To the right, a mom had left a stroller under the trees and was pushing her toddler on the squeaking swings. To my left, a bronzed young woman in a red bikini was working on her suntan, sitting in a camp chair and staring out at the lake through her sunglasses.

How can these people act so lackadaisical? I thought to myself. Don't they know what depravity each of us is capable of? Even the best of us? Dostoevsky's riveting portrait of young Raskolnikov's misguided love for his sister, his insane conviction that he had a special case for committing murder, his compelling rationale for his terrible actions had completely devastated me. Dostoevsky had made me believe that any human being, pushed far enough, could become a Raskolnikov. I looked over at the children playing innocently on the swing, the young woman reclining in her chair, and I shuddered at the murder, rape, and mayhem Dostoevsky had convinced me I was capable of. I remember thinking that this awareness was terrible and wonderful at the same time. I remember thinking *Crime and Punishment* is one of the best novels I have ever read, and I hope I never have to read it again.

A book can be sweet *because* it is devastating. And devastation, though I wouldn't recommend it as a daily ritual, can be one of the most important spurs to spiritual growth. It can bring you face to face with the parts of yourself that you thrust farthest away. And no spiritual life can grow if it refuses to look these parts in the eye. Reading can allow this devastation to happen in a relatively safe place—that is, you can be brought face to face with your own monsters without feeling that you have been forced into this confrontation. You have the choice at any moment to close the book, and the imaginative projection of reading means that you have willingly generated the images of these monsters yourself. This is the case even with books you are required to read for a class: not even a teacher or other authority can supervise your confrontation with these frightening creatures. Nobody is there inside your mind to witness this confron-

tation, which means that you can respond without crafting
that response toward how you will appear before others, and
because of this privacy, your response has the potential to be
honest. I'll have more to say about the importance of privacy in
a minute, but for now, let's move on to other kinds of reading.

FOR I HAVE READ other kinds of books besides the book
of grief and the book of devastation. I have also read books of
great comfort. In fact, I would suggest that one of the great
pleasures of reading is the experience of having confirmed in a
book impulses or instincts that may not yet have become clear
enough to be thoughts. There's a real delight that comes when
some words on the page give clear, concise shape to a morass
of ideas or opinions that you haven't had the opportunity or
stimulus to sort through. Here's an example of one such pleasurable moment of confirmation that I recently experienced. In
his book *The Holy Longing: The Search for a Christian Spirituality*,
Ronald Rolheiser opens his chapter on "Sustaining Ourselves
in the Spiritual Life" with a short line from St. Augustine:
"Knowledge alone cannot save us." I remember looking up
at the world around me after reading this statement. I was in
the backyard on a summer morning, having a quiet time, and
taking great delight in the smell of new evergreen needles in
the two white pines at the back of our property. A woodpecker
was tapping experimentally in the huge oak beyond the pines.

Augustine's statement did not pose a new thought to me,
but I took in a sharp breath anyway when I read this 1,700-year-
old statement because it affirms a belief I hold and that I'm
really glad to have company in holding. I'd have to say that it is
a belief that sometimes makes me feel lonely. I work at a university, and I am constantly reminded that the reason for existence

of universities in our culture is the apprehension and dissemin-
ation of knowledge. Their every value is based on the power
associated with knowledge, and so my gut instinct to distrust
the exclusive power of knowledge to humanize human beings
and to create a better society makes me often feel like a fraud
as a university professor. Because the belief in the inherent
value of knowledge is so powerfully and widely held where
I work, I'm half-convinced of it myself and therefore really
bad at explaining why I distrust it as the main tool of human
improvement. So it's deeply comforting to come across Ronald
Rolheiser, who teaches at St. Michael's College at the University
of Toronto, and Augustine, who also taught at institutions
of higher learning, giving words to my awkward instinct.

My feeling of pleasure is worth analyzing, because it rises
out of the paradox of sociability that I have described in the
earlier chapters as central to spiritual experience. I don't feel
so alone after reading Augustine through Rolheiser. I find
myself in good company. Others have looked at the various
forms of knowledge available to them in their times and
have seen their usefulness, as well as their limits. I'm not
alone in distrusting the acquisition of knowledge by itself as
the road to enlightenment. I've got important friends, like
Augustine and Rolheiser, not to mention Bob the red-bearded
Buddhist postman, Karen Armstrong, and Dionne Brand.
But—and this is why this sociability is paradoxical—this
sense of having friends who think like me happens precisely
when I'm reading by myself words by people who are in fact
very different from me. There's something about my solitude
that opens me up to this unique form of companionship.

Vulnerability is the unique element provided by solitary
reading. Now this vulnerability is obvious in the feeling of

devastation I experienced reading Dostoevsky, but I want to analyze it in more detail in relation to my quieter and much less troubled response to Rolheiser, because I want to show how vulnerability is key, not just in sensational and dramatic moments, but also in subtler ones. I could easily be chatting in a coffee shop and experience a similar feeling of camaraderie if my coffee companion agreed with me that "knowledge alone cannot save us." And I would similarly be relieved by finding that I am not alone in holding this unpopular view. But there's a significant difference in the level at which I can allow myself to be open to an idea or thought in conversation as compared to in solitude. In front of other people, there's always an element of performativity so that the conversation can go forward. We perform the courtesies of listening encouragingly, even if our friends are discussing something that bores us. If they commit errors of courtesy or logic, we give them the benefit of the doubt and don't bring them up short. And we don't pour out all of our insecurities or failings every time we meet, even to friends we trust, because we know that such moments of confession need to be rare if they are to be taken seriously. These are all parts of the art of conversation.

But when we are reading a book, we can open ourselves to the words on the page with impunity. There's an honesty we can allow between ourselves and the page. One level of honesty for me in relation to Augustine's statement is that I think the belief that "knowledge alone cannot save us" can sometimes undermine me as an academic. Because I'm not convinced that having it all figured out, having a completely coherent philosophical system, knowing every last bit of information, would answer my deepest questions and enable me to clear a way to the perfect society or to enlightenment, I am

sometimes lazy about knowledge. I can be undermined by
a distrust in knowledge and therefore not hone my mind to
the nth degree and work out problems with the kind of preci-
sion that I see others produce. I expect that I won't understand
some things, that I have a limited intelligence, and that I will
have to feel my way forward rather than lay it all out in a clear,
systematic explanation. Reading Rolheiser quoting Augustine
by myself lets me admit this without immediately trying to
angle my admission toward a defence. In fact, I am comforted
enough to make this admission at all by knowing about
Rolheiser's and Augustine's companionship in the first place.

In part, this undefended posture is made possible by
the structure of absence. Reading in the absence of physically present witnesses, whether of the author or of others, I
have a feeling of privacy. My readiness to read Augustine's
words in relation to my awkward belonging in the university
and its value system lets me open myself to the possibilities
in his words that I think would not occur in a face-to-face
conversation. A lot of this willingness to be open comes
from my feeling of comfort and security that is one of the
great pleasures of private reading. I can take in a statement, even one that puts a finger on a tender spot, and
not have to defend myself against it from the outset.

BUT READING IS NOT ALWAYS confirmation, as Ezekiel
found out and as did I when I read Dostoevsky. Sometimes,
reading is highly pleasurable because it does the opposite—it
surprises you. This is that feeling when a completely new way
of seeing, an entirely new thought, enables you to make sense
of impulses or experiences that had before remained opaque.
My example of the pleasure of surprise will come, too, from

Rolheiser. I have always distrusted the fierce certitude that characterizes fundamentalist forms of religion, and, when I came across Rolheiser's reformulation of what prayer is, I felt a profound relief and delight in understanding why I've always held that distrust. Rolheiser says prayer is much more than a series of requests, or even a conversation with God. Instead, he insists that prayer is a specific form of pondering, a form that involves a patient bearing of tension. "To ponder, biblically," he writes, "is to stand before life's great mysteries the way Mary stood before the various events of Jesus' life, including the way she stood under the cross" (Rolheiser 220). Rolheiser goes on to explain that this is what constitutes nobility of soul. "Usually we ascribe that quality," he says, "to the person who, mindless of his or her own comfort, need, and pain, is willing for a higher reason to carry a great tension for a long period of time, not acquiescing to the temptation to prematurely resolve things" (221). He goes on to suggest that the willingness to carry tension is a sign of great respect, for it allows others to be themselves without demanding that they resolve one's own concerns; it is also a mysterious mode of gestation, which turns hurt into healing, wound into supple flesh, and discord into friendship.

I read this passage the same day I read Rolheiser's quotation from Augustine, and, as I sat in my lawn chair in the backyard, smelling the bracing evergreen scent of the pines, I felt a thrill of discovery run through me. Rolheiser's idea was entirely new to me. I had felt beforehand that wisdom doesn't rush to conclusions and that people with big souls are not people who hurry to solutions. I had been offended by zealots who had answers to others' questions, even before they asked them. And I had known that prayer is more than mouthing a set of demands and more, even, than "talking with God." But

I had never before thought of prayer as a kind of pondering that is rooted in a character quality—one that is willing to live in unresolved tension. As soon as I read it, however, I thrust my fist in the air and shouted out, "Of course! That's right!" A tingle ran through my whole body. I had never thought of tension in such positive terms, and I had never understood prayer to be so practically engaged. More than this, I realized why I intuitively respect people who, now that I see it, know how to carry tension productively and patiently. I realized why I have felt this kind of respect for such people, some of whom come from other religious traditions from my own and some of whom are not religious at all. And I also see why I feel disappointed in myself when I break out from under tensions that are parts of my life and try to force early resolutions.

In a way, my experience of surprise is like an experience of confirmation in the sense that the rightness of Rolheiser's statement applies accurately to explain things I had only intuited before. It is as though his surprising statement confirmed something I had not yet known but that I had the readiness to know. Again, my sense of his having given me the gift of this helpful way of seeing things felt like friendship, like encountering a companion along the road. It made me feel not so much alone, as I sat reading, by myself, in my backyard.

ALL THESE STORIES OF READING, whether of devastating Dostoevsky or of confirming Augustine or of surprising Rolheiser, are individualistic stories, featuring me with my own thoughts in the park or in the backyard. This private context makes it tempting to examine the effects of reading through the lens of psychotherapy, to think that the importance of eating the book of sorrows, for example, is all about

the therapeutic effect of acknowledging in story and word the
broken and hurtful elements of our private, hidden lives. I have
no wish to downplay the importance of the potential healing
that can happen when we see our individual sorrows acknowledged in print, but Ezekiel the book-eater wasn't being called,
exactly, to become a psychotherapist. He was being called to be
a prophet, an activist-protestor to exiles that had lost their own
story and their own values. I have said that one reason he was
given a book of grief to eat in preparation for his work, besides
the fact that it would make him accustomed to the grief of
being ignored by his audience, was that sorrow has the potential to bypass the defences of the proud intellect. And I have
said that the experience of devastation can be sweet as honey
because, although it feels like jackboots on the soul, it can make
you self-aware in a remarkably powerful, life-transforming way.

There is also a sweetness and satisfaction, however, not
on the level of personal psychology, but on the level of the
social and political, that occurs when the sad truth is told.
This is a very important point because it seems to me that
one of the trickiest parts to describe in this book's meditation
on spirituality and reading is how reading can be something
beyond a self-engrossing activity. Recall the common-sense
dismissals in which people will say "it's all book-learnin'
and ain't got no practical sense" or she's got her "head in
the clouds and is no earthly good." But there are ways in
which eating the book can open us up to cultural politics,
to the real social and political worlds in which we live.

Let me give several examples. The first one is from Dennis
Lee, the Canadian poet, who describes how he experienced
four years of writer's block during the years of the Vietnam
War. At that time he felt that all the words and poetic forms he

could think of to describe Canada in the shadow of America rang false. There was a kind of "cadence," he said, a kind of heartbeat or rhythm to Canadian life that he sensed but just couldn't put a finger on. Everything he knew how to write—sonnets, epics, free verse, odes, satires, metaphors, allegories, irony, paradox—they all seemed inadequate. He was at an impasse, and he found himself blocked for four long years.

Then, he chanced upon and ate a book of sorrow. It was George Grant's *Lament for a Nation*. There, Lee said, he finally came upon an account for the failure of Canada, for its failure to follow its founding instincts to chart a radically different course from the United States in North America. Grant assesses Canada's failure to found a society where something other than material acquisition, unlimited capital expansion, and blind faith in the benefits of technology ruled the country. He laments the lost potential where a limited constitutional monarchy insisted that the role of government was to protect the populace from the limitless greed of technologized capitalism. Canadians love to think of Canada as innocent of the greater sins of the United States, to imagine that we have treated Indigenous peoples more justly, that we have developed more humane systems of public administration, such as free healthcare and an official multiculturalism policy. Especially during the years of the Vietnam War when Canada was the destination for draft resisters from the United States, we congratulated ourselves as a country of peace lovers. Grant's book of sorrows flew in the face of this self-congratulation. It lamented Canada's inability to keep from becoming a branch plant of the American Empire (including its participation in the weapons industry during Vietnam), and Dennis

Lee, strangely, found in Grant's jeremiad an honest expression of the Canadian experience that he had been unable to name.

The point I wish to make here is not about whether or not we agree with Grant's assessment of Canada's complex relationship with the United States, but about what happened to one reader, Dennis Lee, when he read this particular book of sorrows. In finding this book, Lee says that he felt an enormous satisfaction at the honesty of Grant's assessment, and that, having been given this sad story of failure, he found a way to give voice to a Canadian heartbeat (Lee, "Cadence" 511, 517). A story of failure, read all alone by himself, helped him identify a public rhythm he had sensed but couldn't name. The book of Canadian sorrows, honestly written, was sweet as honey for Lee, for it satisfied the longing he had felt, neither for platitudes or clever answers nor for covering over and avoiding the disappointments of Canadian history. He needed the lamentations, wailings, and moanings to be told. And when that longing was met, his writer's block ended; he got a finger on the country's cadence, its pulse, and the words began to flow again. In fact, they became his own book of lamentations, a collection of poems called *Civil Elegies and Other Poems* that won the Governor General's award in 1973. In this book he wrote:

> what can anyone do in this country, baffled and
> making our penance for ancestors, what did they leave us?
>   Indian-swindlers, ‹
> stewards of unclaimed earth and rootless what does it matter
>   if they, our
> forebears' flesh and bone were often
> good men, good men do not matter to history.

And what can we do here now, for at last we have no notion
of what we might have come to be in America, alternative.
(*from "Elegy 1,"* Civil Elegies *28*)

His testimony continues with its mix of sorrow and confession, one that remains powerfully relevant, from the napalm of Vietnam to the depleted uranium scattered across the landscapes of Bosnia, Serbia, and Iraq:

In a bad time, people, from an outpost of empire I write
bewildered, though on about living. It is to set down a nation's
failure of nerve; I mean complicity, which is signified by the
gaseous stain above us. For a man who
fries the skin of kids with burning jelly is a
criminal. Even though he loves children he is a criminal. Even
      though his
money pumps your oil he is criminal, and though his programs invest
      the air you breathe he is
criminal and though his honest quislings run your
government he is criminal and though you do not love his enemies
      he is
criminal and though you lose your job on his say-so he is criminal and
      though he has
transformed the categories of your refusal by the pressure of his media
      he is a criminal.
And the consenting citizens of a minor and docile colony
are cogs in a useful tool, though in no way
necessary and scarcely
criminal at all and their leaders are
honourable men.
(*from "Elegy 5" 41*)

Like Ezekiel, Jeremiah, and St. John, Dennis Lee ate a book of grief, and, despite its bitter contents, it tasted sweet as honey. It connected him with the cadence he had sensed but been unable to put a finger on. Like eight-year-old Dionne Brand, leaning over the mahogany drawer in her grandmother's house, he fell into the face of a book, and that book was a mirror and an ocean. It showed him his own self, and it showed him himself immersed in a history that is at once terrifying and affirming—terrifying because it is a history of inhumanity and genocide, but affirming because it gave him an honest picture free of self justifying illusions, and this honest picture gave him a role, a channel for what had been instinctual and inarticulate. He found his voice.

My second example of how reading reaches beyond the personal to affect cultural politics comes from the experiences of Protestant literacy teachers in southern Ethiopia. I mentioned Ato Markina Meja in chapter three, the man who was asked by the church elders back in the 1930s to show he could read the Bible in Amharic in order to qualify for baptism. His autobiography and that of an evangelist teacher from Gomo Gofa named Ato Mehari Choramo provide dramatic instances of the important role literacy played in generating a whole new set of social and political arrangements in the regions of Walaitta and Gomo Gofa. It is striking, in both of these men's autobiographies, how much time they spent in prison for their faith. In order to understand why, we need to remember that the people of these regions were colonized by the Christian Orthodox Amhara people during the nineteenth century. Central to this colonial system was the imposition of the Orthodox faith upon these largely animistic people. So, when Protestant Christianity began to

spread through the efforts of people such as Ato Markina
and Ato Mehari, it was seen as a threat to the dominance of
the Amharic-Orthodox ruling class. Again and again, these
teachers were thrown into prison and beaten, while the fledg-
ling, grass-roofed churches they had built were burnt to
the ground. Ato Mehari, for example, reports that he was
arrested and interrogated at least twelve times throughout
his career. He was shackled, beaten up, and left for months
at a time in down-country police stations, often desperately sick from the abuse he received and from lack of food.

So what did these men teach and why was it so threatening?
They taught two things: that the way of Jesus was open to
all regardless of race, caste, gender, or class and that a person
needed to read in order to learn about this way. These men
received meagre financial support from their home churches
in Walaitta and Gomo Gofa, so they made the majority of their
income by teaching Amharic literacy classes in the villages
in which they settled. Ato Markina reports that, during the
1930s when the Italian occupation of Ethiopia made teaching
materials hard to find, he made ink from the fruit of the
ketchemo tree and nibs from bamboo. With these crude instru-
ments, and with a whiteboard he fashioned out of unbleached
cotton stretched over a piece of wood, he taught 250 eager
students their letters in one village alone. Evangelist-teachers
like him and Ato Mehari did this in village after village until a
significant number of Walaittans and Gomo Gofans could read.

These readers composed a new populace in these outlying
provinces that was harder for the Amhara governors to subju-
gate. In order to understand the new faith, interested people
learned to read and write. This literacy made them individuals who understood their roles in the community in a whole

new way. They no longer depended so heavily on what others told them, what decrees governors or priests made, or what inherited tradition held to be self-evident. As Martin Luther's campaign for independent Bible-reading had predicted four hundred years earlier in Germany, literacy among these Ethiopians was foundational to personal faith, which in turn produced newly empowered citizens. So, for example, people who became literate believers no longer feared either *qallichas*, diviners, or *fugas*, people believed to have the evil eye. The *qallichas*, with their occult knowledge of the connection between spirits and physical health, held the rest of the populace in such fear that even the Amhara governors were afraid to approach them to collect taxes. You never knew what kind of spell a *qallicha* would cast upon you if you vexed him. Sometimes the newly literate Protestants' independence made them useful to the powers of the time, and Ato Mehari reports that, because these readers had no fear of *qallichas,* one governor used them to collect taxes from a widely feared *qallicha.*

But these literate believers were more often troublesome to the status quo. For instance, *fugas* were artisans who worked as potters, blacksmiths, wood-carvers, or makers of leather goods, but they were feared and therefore despised. Even though they were necessary to every community, their ability to see shape, colour, and structure made people fear they had supernatural visual powers. Suspecting they had the evil eye, people would never invite *fugas* into their homes, nor would anyone eat the food they had prepared. If a *fuga* looked at a baby, everyone knew it would soon grow sick and die. Believers like Ato Mehari dispensed with these superstitions and welcomed *fugas* into their fellowship, shared meals with them, and thus incurred the wrath of many of their neighbours. The independent thinking of this group of readers threw the whole system of social status into disarray.

Even more troubling to the colonial rulers, however, was the fact that literate believers could use the colonial system itself to resist the local governors who represented it. Ato Markina reports that around 1961 the Walaitta believers grew exasperated with the constant harassment from the Amhara-Orthodox authorities. The arrests, the beatings of literacy teachers, the interrogations of young church members, and the burning of churches had risen to an intolerable rate, so the church leaders in the region met to discuss what they should do. Let us take a moment to imagine the situation. Despite being persecuted, the Walaitta and Gomo Gofa Protestant churches had steadily expanded since the 1930s. Most of the members of these new communities came from the peasant class in Emperor Haile Selassie's feudal society. So they eked out their livings from small grain farms and a few cows and chickens, and every harvest season, the wealthy landlords in Addis Ababa sent share-collectors, with an armed escort if necessary, to seize their portion of the peasants' produce. It had been this way for at least a hundred years. Any time the peasants expressed dissatisfaction with the system, they lost out either in court or at the end of a policeman's nightstick. These rural peasants had no recourse. They were a colonized people whose lives were utterly controlled by an impenetrable system of Amhara law, Amhara religion, and Amhara force. Then, in a relatively short period of time, tireless workers like Ato Mehari and Ato Markina produced a literate peasant class. Their purposes were not consciously political. They just wanted people to be able to understand about the way of Jesus and to be able to read its basic statements for themselves. But readers are harder to

manipulate than non-readers. And so, despite the apolitical
intentions of the evangelists, they created a new political force.

The new church leaders met together to decide what they
could do about the constant harassment from the Amhara
governors. Because they were able to read, they realized that the
governors were operating in contradiction to the new Ethiopian
constitution, which declared freedom of religion regardless of
ethnicity, race, or region. So, next time a church was closed and
the teacher was arrested, the leaders sent a delegation to the
provincial governor to insist upon their legal right to freedom
of religion, and when he refused to hear their case, they sent a
delegation to Addis Ababa, the capital city, where they placed
a petition before the Amhara-Orthodox king, Haile Selassie.

Because they were able to read and write, they could read
constitutions and sign petitions. And, because they were part
of the new movement of Christians, they became acquainted
with city Protestants who included legal experts among their
numbers. So they consulted with these legal experts, who
advised them to establish an "Evangel Fellowship Association"
with other Protestant church groups and to register themselves with the ministry of the Interior to become a legally
recognized corporation. While they were in the city, the
down-country Protestants also decided to raise money for
a piece of land in Addis where a central office and a guest-
house could be built so that, when new problems arose in
their provinces, they could make quick contact with the
central government. Having established these measures,
the Walaitta and Gomo Gofa church leaders returned to
their homes with a new ability to protect themselves and
other peasants from the abuses of their local governors.

⦂ THESE ETHIOPIAN EXAMPLES of how reading enables cultural politics help us from Western cultures to witness afresh the process of radical change that is beyond our memories. Most people in Europe and North America don't remember what it was like to gain access to the culture of literacy for the first time. But some people have not forgotten. During the 1930s a remarkable program called the Federal Writer's Project, concerned that the generation of African Americans who had experienced slavery would soon be dead, gathered former slaves' experiences of learning to read. As Alberto Manguel describes it in *A History of Reading,* the background to this project reaches back to a 1660 decree by Charles II that the Council for Foreign Plantations should instruct natives, servants, and slaves of the British colonies in the precepts of Christianity. Manguel reports that the decree raised a furor among slave-owners who realized that if slaves were taught to read the Bible, they would eventually encounter inflammatory notions of their own humanity and develop ambitions for revolt and freedom. They might anticipate the call of Toussaint L'Ouverture. Opposition to Charles's decree was strongest in the colonies where there were the largest populations of slaves, so South Carolina, for example, passed strict laws in the 1700s forbidding all Blacks, whether slave or free, from learning to read. These laws stayed in effect until well into the nineteenth century.

The Federal Writers' Project interviewed people who had lived their young lives under these laws. Belle Myers said that she had learned her letters from watching the plantation owner's baby play with alphabet blocks, and when her master realized what she was doing, he kicked her with his boots. Doc Daniel Dowdy recalled that "the first time you was caught trying to read or write you was whipped with a cowhide, the next time with a cat-o-nine tails and the third time they cut the first joint off your fore-finger." Throughout the South it was common for slave-owners to hang any slave who taught others to read (Manguel 280). Reading was a threat to the whole economy of slavery, for it qualified people who had been excluded from the category of humanity to be known as human, as intelligent individuals, as people with agency and minds of their own (see Gates). Even though few of us in twenty-first-century Europe or North America went through extreme experiences such as these in the transition from being non-readers to becoming readers, all readers have gone through a radical change. For most of us, that change took place at an early age when nearly everything was changing dramatically every day for us anyway, so we may not have noticed how powerful a change it was. Perhaps people who have encountered literacy later in life, or those who have achieved it against powerful odds, can help us remember how truly life-empowering it is to become a reader.

Stories like those gathered in the Federal Writers' Project or recounted by Ato Mehari and Ato Marltina show by contrast how, for many of us, reading is blasé, taken for granted and even easily dismissed. Or, if it's not dismissed, it's minimized by being personalized. By this I mean that we tend to think of the personal and private benefits of reading and, in so doing, we forget the wide-ranging social and political effects it has. We tend to psychologize reading—and spirituality, too, for that matter—and fail to see one of the central points I have been trying to emphasize, which is that eating the book is not solely an exercise to feed one's inner life. Rather, eating the book— not just nibbling at it, or having a little taste here and there, but eating it wholesale—produces a changed person, an empowered person, a different kind of person; and changed people means social and political change, too, not just personal change.

A dramatic instance of the kind of change wrought by literacy that is simultaneously personal and political can be seen in the life story of David George, who was born into slavery in Essex County, Virginia, around 1743, and who learned to read the Bible from his master's children when he was a young adult. In 1773 he co-founded Silver Bluff Baptist Church in Silver Bluff, Georgia, the first Black church in North America. Think about this: the system of slavery is founded upon the belief that African-descended people are not humans of the same order as White people, that they can be exploited for labour because they do not have the spiritual or mental capacities for full membership in "Christian civilization." The founding of a Black church insists that Black people have souls, that they, too, are children of God. When George and the others established Silver Bluffs, they flew in the face of the whole political and economic system of the plantation economy. George went on to join the Black Loyalist forces in Savannah, Georgia, after the Dunmore proclamation of 1775, according to which the British promised liberty to any slaves who joined the British side during the Revolutionary War. After the British loss, George and the other Black allies of the Crown were given grants of land in Nova Scotia, where, just in case we dream of Canada as the promised land of liberty and justice for escaping slaves, he raised the hatred of White settlers with his preaching and baptizing of Black and White converts alike. Perhaps a Black preacher can shepherd the souls of Black people, but the idea that an ex-slave should oversee the spiritual lives of White people was so unacceptable to people in Shelburne, Nova Scotia, that his church was tipped over on its side, and his house, along with others in the Black neighbourhood where he lived, was vandalized and burned. Eventually, after several years of White persecution, George joined the large contingent of Black Loyalists who departed Nova Scotia for Sierra Leone in 1792.

But let us pause for a moment on what David George has to say about the process of learning to read back in Silver Bluff:

> Then I got a spelling book and began to read. As Master was a
> great man, he kept a White school-master to teach the White
> children to read. I used to go to the little children to teach me
> a, b, c. They would give me a lesson, which I tried to learn,
> and then I would go to them again, and ask if I was right?
> The reading so ran in my mind, that I think I learned in
> my sleep as really as when I was awake; and I can now read
> the Bible, so that what I have in my heart, I can see
> again in the Scriptures." (George 34, my emphasis)

I find this final statement fascinating and important, especially for the closing pages of my book on the spirituality and cultural politics of reading. There may be a temptation to read this book as an insistence on the priority of reading for developing a spiritual life. As I hope I have made clear, I do think reading can play a powerful role in developing a person's capacity for attentiveness, for openness and vulnerability toward the Other, and that these are essential qualities for a spirituality that has dynamic effects in the practical world. But George's wording here is key: he already had his thoughts, his impulses, his convictions, and what he saw, when he learned to read the Scriptures, was confirmation or clarification of them. His was a pleasure of confirmation. Crossing the structure of absence, an absence enforced by the anti-literacy laws of slavery-era America, his was an affirmation that he had a mind, that his convictions were sound, that he was a person, that he had a soul, that his words carried weight, had power, could change the world. He already had a spirituality. Reading is not the only way to spiritual life, nor is it somehow essential to it. But reading what he already knew privately empowered him publicly, gave him agency in the world. Literacy transformed his inner perceptions and convictions into cultural politics. It simultaneously alienated him from the world around him, made him a freak both to illiterate slaves and enraged Whites. Just like the eight-year-old girl, it lifted him out of the world he knew—literally, right out of the South and into Canada, then Africa. And it put him into a new world, a new perception of himself in the world, a new series of communities, first Silver Bluff Baptist Church, then Shelburne Baptist Church, next the community of free Blacks who made the journey to Sierra Leone, and then the abolitionists who recorded his narrative. Reading played a key role in transforming his individual impulse into public, collective power.

⠿ MY PURPOSE IN THIS BOOK has been to try to defamiliarize a wonderfully powerful process that we can take too much for granted. I want to encourage all of us to re-think our relationship to reading and to renovate our reading habits, which can be deadened by over-familiarity. Reading can be much more than an instrumental process by which we simply acquire information, much more than an escapist activity by which we entertain ourselves. Reading can do these things, but it can also be nourishing for our spiritual lives, and when it is, it can reinvigorate our cultural politics. We can see the signal contribution reading can make to spirituality in the way that the major religions put books at the centre of their practices. When we worship, when we pray, when we meditate, when we wish to reach out beyond our egos to a new awareness of others, of the world around us, of God—we often do so by the aid of a book. We do this because reading is a process that simultaneously *individualizes* us by placing the words on the page between us and the world and *connects* us by drawing us out of ourselves through imaginative projection toward the thoughts and experiences of others. At one and the same time, reading is a technology of alienation and a maker of new community. In order for us to be nourished by this double process, we must develop right posture toward the books we read. If we are to do better than simply amass knowledge from books and then use that knowledge to show that we know more than other people, we need to open ourselves to the otherness of the book. We need to become vulnerable to the voice of the Other in the book. We need to learn a discerning attentiveness so that the voice in the book can do more than echo back to us our own pre-existing views. If we are to be changed by a book, we must consume it deliberately and slowly, allowing ourselves to taste its many flavours, whether sweet or sour, whether confirming or devastating, whether full of comfort or full of pain. By so doing we can let our experiences of reading teach us about the cultural politics in spirituality—about the ways in which we are connected to others, to God, and to the world beyond ourselves.

Reading can give us practice in important spiritual disciplines: it can help us develop our capacity for attention, it can increase our ability to listen, and it can help us develop mental organization and alertness. Reading can draw us out of ourselves and can give us practice in listening to the less-obvious that's always going on around us. It can give us daily experience in reaching across the structure of absence so that we learn to read the present signs of the Other even in the Other's absence and, by that means, to put ourselves in contact with communities that would not be available in our own time and place.

Some of the people who have had the most profound impact on my life are people I have never met and never expect to. Fyodor Dostoevsky, Thich Nhat Hanh, Macrina Wiederkehr, Shams ud-din Muhammed Hafiz, Ngugi wa Thiong'o, Ronald Rolheiser, Paulo Friere, Ato Mehari, Mary Oliver, David the Psalmist, St. Augustine—I've never met any of them, but they have become companions, advisors, confidants in my ongoing journey. All of them are literally absent, and all of them intimately present to my process of understanding who I am, where I am going, where I live, what time it is, and what the world looks like. All of them are people who have cast signs upon the page, indications of how they lived in the world, how humans are connected to one another, and what possibilities there are for us to make sense of ourselves, to make communities that are life-giving, or to embody love and justice in the world.

Although reading, to some degree, produces me as an individual because it helps me, like it did St. Ambrose in the fourth century, to have an inner dialogue by myself, it also reminds me that I'm not an autonomous individual, that I am interdependent with others. For, reading is a process of intimate mental projection into the mind of another where each of us makes contact with what Don McKay calls the "companionable ghost," that other breath that breathes within our breath. Furthermore, reading reminds us that even this feeling of intimacy is heavily mediated: the words

I am reading on the page are not direct emanations from the things and ideas themselves. They are signs that stand in for what's not present. They make sense because people generally agree about what they mean, and they come to me by means of translators, editors, publishers, and booksellers.

Awareness of these levels of mediation is central to spiritual experience because, first, it keeps us from engulfing the Other. It maintains the otherness of the Other because the Other is physically removed from us in the moment of contact; it reminds us of the limits of our desire for and understanding of the Other. Second, it reminds us that the Creator has chosen to communicate with human beings through this heavily mediated means, through the words, experiences, and gestures of other living beings. God trusts human beings to embody the divine in the world. Whatever we know about the life of the spirit comes to us through our ability and willingness to pay attention to the books we have been given: the books of God, the books by other people, the book of nature, the continually being-written books of our own lives.

So, like the little boy in bed with the Word, even before we actually start to read the words from the page, we need a posture of expectancy, a posture of quiet, a posture that is fuelled by longing for connection. Like the violinist or singer who picks up the sheet of music, we cannot remain passive. We must perform the text to bring it to life. We must project across the structure of absence to produce a lively connection with the Creator, as well as with other mediators and performers of the text. And finally, like the boy on the rabbi's lap, we need to eat the books we have been given. We need to consume them wholly, fully, and slowly, so that they become parts of our bodies, the very structure of our lives.

For reading can give us a role to play, a direction for our energies, a way to channel our spiritual hunger that takes us into the social and political worlds in which we live. Because it does this, we will find that even books of sorrow, even books of devastation, along with books of surprise and books of confirmation, can be books that taste sweet as honey.

REFERENCES

Anonymous. *The Cloud of Unknowing*. Ed. William Johnson. New York: Doubleday, 1973.

Armstrong, Karen. *The Spiral Staircase: My Climb Out of Darkness*. Toronto: Vintage Canada, 2005.

Augustine. *On Christian Doctrine*. Trans. D.W. Robertson, Jr. Upper Saddle River, NJ: Prentice Hall, 1958.

Barthes, Roland. "From Work to Text." *The Critical Tradition*. Ed. David H. Richter. New York: Bedford/St. Martin's Press, 1989. 1005–10.

Booth, Wayne. *The Company We Keep: An Ethics of Fiction*. Berkeley: University of California Press, 1988.

Brand, Dionne. *A Map to the Door of No Return: Notes to Belonging*. Toronto: Doubleday Canada, 2001.

Casey, Michael. *Sacred Reading: The Ancient Art of* Lectio Divina. Liguori, MO: Liguori/Triumph, 1995.

Cotterell, F. Peter. *Born at Midnight*. Chicago: Moody Press, 1973.

Davidson, Donald. "Radical Interpretation." *Inquiries into Truth and Interpretation*. Oxford: Clarendon, 1984.

de Caussade, Jean-Pierre. *The Sacrament of the Present Moment*. Trans. Kitty Muggeridge. San Francisco: HarperSanFrancisco,1981.

Derrida, Jacques. "Structure, Sign, and Play in the Discourse of the Human Sciences." *The Critical Tradition*. Ed. David H. Richter. New York: Bedford/St. Martin's Press, 1989. 959–971.

Felman, Shoshana. "Turning the Screw of Interpretation." In *Literature and Psychoanalysis: The Question of Reading: Otherwise*. Ed. Shoshana

Felman. Baltimore and London: Johns Hopkins University Press, 1977, 1980. 94–207.

Gates, Henry Louis Jr. "Writing, 'Race,' and the Difference It Makes." *The Critical Tradition*. 2nd ed. Ed. David Richter. New York: Bedford, 1998. 1575–88.

George, David. "An account of the Life of Mr. David George, from Sierra Leone in Africa; given by himself in a Conversation with Brother Rippon in London, and Brother Pearce of Birmingham." (1793). In *Fire on the Water: An Anthology of Black Nova Scotian Writing*. Ed. George Elliott Clarke. Vol. 1. Lawrencetown Beach, NS: Pottersfield Press, 1991. 32–39.

Grant, George. *Lament for a Nation: The Defeat of Canadian Nationalism* (1965). Ottawa: Carlton University Press, 1995.

Hafiz (Shams-ud-din Muhammad Hafiz). *The Gift: Poems by Hafiz the Great Sufi Master*. Trans. Daniel Ladinsky. New York: Penguin, 1999.

Hanh, Thich Nhat. *A Lifetime of Peace: Essential Writings by and about Thich Nhat Hanh*. Ed. Jennifer Schwamm Willis. New York: Marlowe and Co., 2003.

Jacobs, Alan. *A Theology of Reading: The Hermeneutics of Love*. Cambridge, MA: Westview Press, 2001.

Jeffrey, David Lyle. *People of the Book: Christian Identity and Literary Culture*. Grand Rapids, MI: William B. Eerdmans, 1996.

Lee, Dennis. "Cadence, Country, Silence: Writing in Colonial Space." 1984. In *Towards a Canadian Literature: Essays, Editorials and Manifestos*. Ed. Douglas M. Daymond and Leslie G. Monkman. Vol. 2, 1940–1983. Ottawa: Tecumseh Press, 1985. 497–520.

———. *Civil Elegies and Other Poems*. Toronto: House of Anansi Press, 1972.

Malone, Nancy M. *Walking a Literary Labyrinth: A Spirituality of Reading*. New York: Riverhead Books, 2003.

Manguel, Alberto. *A History of Reading*. Toronto: Alfred A. Knopf Canada, 1996.

Markina Meja. *The Autobiography of Markina Meja*. Trans. Haile Jenai. Addis Ababa, 2001. Unpublished manuscript.

McKay, Don. "Wings of Song." In *Another Gravity*. Toronto: McClelland and Stewart, 2000. 47.

Mehari Choramo. *Ethiopian Revivalist: The Autobiography of Evangelist Mehari Choramo.* Trans. and annotated by Brian Farger. Edmonton: Enterprise Publishers, 1997.

Muhammed the Prophet. *Meaning of the Qur'ân: The Last Testament and Final Revelation on Earth.* Trans. Abdullah Yusuf Ali. Scarborough, ON: Al-Attique Publishers, 2003.

Pascal, Blaise. *Pensées.* #43. Trans. W. F. Trotter. New York: The Modern Library, 1941.

Pennington, M. Basil. *A Place Apart: Monastic Prayer and Practice for Everyone.* Garden City, NY: Doubleday, 1983.

Peterson, Eugene H. *Eat This Book: A Conversation in the Art of Spiritual Reading.* Grand Rapids, MI, and Cambridge, UK: William B. Eerdmans, 2006.

Plato. *Phaedrus.* In *The Works of Plato.* Trans. Benjamin Jowett. Ed. Irwin Edman. New York: The Modern Library, 1956. 263–329.

Poulet, Georges. "Criticism and the Experience of Interiority." Trans. Catherine and Richard Macksey. *Reader-Response Criticism: From Formalism to Post-Structuralism.* Ed. Jane P. Tompkins. Baltimore and London: Johns Hopkins University Press, 1980. 41–49.

Ricoeur, Paul. *Freud and Philosophy: An Essay on Interpretation.* Trans. Denis Savage. New Haven and London: Yale University Press, 1970.

Rolheiser, Ronald. *The Holy Longing: The Search for a Christian Spirituality.* New York: Doubleday, 1999.

Scarry, Elaine. *Dreaming by the Book.* Princeton, NJ: Princeton University Press, 1999.

Smith, Paul. *Discerning the Subject.* Minneapolis: University of Minnesota Press, 1988.

Steiner, George. *Real Presences.* Chicago: University of Chicago Press, 1989.

Suskind, Ron. "Without a Doubt." *New York Times Magazine.* Saturday, October 17, 2004. Available at: *www.ronsuskind.com/articles/000106.html.* Accessed December 19, 2008.

Weil, Simone. *Waiting on God.* Trans. Emma Crawford. 5th ed. London: Collins, 1969.

Wiederkehr, Macrina, OSB. *A Tree Full of Angels: Seeing the Holy in the Ordinary.* San Francisco: HarperSanFrancisco, 1988.

INDEX